D0620037

HOW TO
Protect
THOSE YOU
Love

By Praying the
Armor of God Daily

HOW TO
Protect
THOSE YOU
Love

By Praying the
Armor of God Daily

RICK STEDMAN

Dedication

To Gay Stedman

Long before seatbelts, God created mothers. One of my earliest memories is of my mother serving as a human, maternal seatbelt, protecting hcr children before seatbelts were mandatory in cars. Whenever our car suddenly slowed down or stopped, her arm was already across the lap of whichever child was sitting beside her—*thwump*—holding us safely in place.

In fact, as I reflect on my life, in hindsight I can see that my mother's entire adult life has been an attempt to protect and prosper the lives of her three children and eight grandchildren. It is an honor, therefore, to dedicate this book about protecting our loved ones to my mother, Gay Stedman, who has spent her life doing just that.

Table of Contents

Chapter One

How Do We Protect Ourselves and Those We Love?

"Leave no unguarded place,
No weakness of the soul,
Take every virtue, every grace,
And fortify the whole."
— Wesley

Is it possible, in this twisted, treacherous world, to protect both ourselves and our loved ones against evil?

A few years ago I was driving Jesse, my then 14-year-old son, home from school. Like every other parent on the planet, I asked, "How was school today?" My son casually replied, "School was okay— except my TA [Teaching Assistant] in English was stoned." Trying not to seem shocked, I said, "Wow! What do you think about that?"

A little background here might be helpful. Jesse is the youngest of my three kids. He began school in a Christian kindergarten and attended a Christian school throughout his elementary and junior high school years. All his friends were Christian kids from Christian families. I fully expected he'd attend and then graduate from a

Christian high school, but God had other plans. At a summer camp a few weeks after his eighth grade graduation, Jesse and his older brother Noah became convicted that they were not witnessing enough for Christ, and they felt God leading them to enroll at the local, public high school. They wanted to influence other kids and make an eternal difference in their lives.

My wife and I were very impressed with this decision and their discernment of God's call. Though we were extremely wary because of the drug-infested reputation of the local high school, Amy and I agreed after praying and seeking insight from God's Word.

So what was I to do? Here was my son in class, exposed to someone—the Teacher's Assistant, no less—who was stoned on pot. Should we yank him out of school to protect him from temptation? Should I talk to the teacher? The Principal? The Governor? The President? (My emotions were getting carried away a bit.)

Once I regained my focus, I assumed the best way to proceed was to just ask more questions. So I calmly asked, "Is this the first time that's happened?"

Jesse responded, "No, he's a real stoner, and he smokes pot every day."

I asked, "Do other kids do drugs at your high school?"

He said, "Of course."

Finally, I nervously asked the question, "How about you? Have you ever tried drugs or felt a desire to try them?"

To my delight, he responded, "No way. Doing drugs is dumb. Those kids are idiots."

At that moment, I was both elated and scared. I was elated

he was standing strong against temptations and that he and I were having this conversation! How better to talk about such issues while he was still at home, rather than have him be forced to deal with these alone when he later would be away from home at college or at a job. During the rest of the drive home, we continued to talk about drugs, temptation, and peer pressure. It was a fantastic day for me as a dad.

But I was also scared. How could I, as a father, protect my son in a public school environment? I couldn't be physically present with him nor consult him in the moment. I couldn't get rid of all temptations. So what could I do? How could I keep my son safe in a world of moral danger?

I'm sure that most parents share this concern. How can we protect our children against the onslaught of a "perverse and sinful generation"? (Mark 8:38, KJV) How can we defend ourselves and those we love against the "flaming arrows" of the enemy? (Ephesians 6:16) But these questions don't apply just to parents. How can married couples protect themselves from the incredible temptations that bombard them in modern culture? How can grandparents, neighbors, singles or classmates protect their families and friends from the enemy who seeks "to kill and destroy"? (John 10:10) Honestly, our human defenses are no match for this enemy. How can we possibly protect ourselves and our loved ones?

Fortunately, the Apostle Paul answers this question in Ephesians 6:11: "Put on the full armor of God so that you can take your stand against the devil's schemes." Paul's solution is clear: we protect ourselves and our loved ones by putting on the full armor of God.

13

For most Christians, however, this answer raises a more difficult question: Just *how* does one put on the full armor of God? Paul says to do it, but doesn't mention how. For many years I tried to put this armor on myself.

I tried to be truthful, to be peaceful, to be righteous, etc. I'm sure you can guess the result. In spite of my sincere efforts, I would fail repeatedly.

Then it hit me that since this is the armor of God, it probably was not something I could put on myself. If I were to successfully put on the armor of God, I would need God to put it on and in me. So rather than *trying* to be truthful, peaceful, and righteous, I began to ask God to *clothe* and *fill* me with his truth, his peace, his righteousness, etc.

In other words, I began to *pray* the armor of God.

How to Put on the Armor of God? Pray!

In fact, this is how Paul ends this section of his letter to the Ephesians. He wrote in verse 18, "And pray in the Spirit on all occasions with all kinds of prayers and requests. With this in mind, be alert and always keep on praying for all the saints." In other words, he too says, "Keep praying about it."

This was a thrilling insight for me personally, and I began to pray the armor of God with gusto. At first, I began to pray through the whole armor of God every day: for myself, for my family members (one at a time), for my friends, for my church, and for the world. But this was overwhelming; the topics were too important and too diverse to cover quickly. I learned that the list of six items was too much for me to adequately pray for each day, so I began to focus on one piece of armor per day. I found this to be more manageable and enjoyable.

There was one problem: I would sometimes forget which piece of armor I prayed for on the previous day, so I would start the list over at the beginning. Over time, I saw that I was praying more often for the belt of truth than the helmet of salvation or the sword of the Spirit. Then I noticed that, In Ephesians 6:13-18 there were six pieces to the armor of God, plus the instruction to "…pray in the spirit on all occasions." I realized that these seven topics would pair nicely with the seven days of the week. After a bit of work, I was able to match the seven items with a simple phrase whose first letter corresponded with the day of the week. Finally, I developed the following list as a simple memory device to help me and our church members remember which piece of armor to pray each day. If you have already memorized the days of the week, then you can easily memorize and utilize the armor of God in prayer!

Sunday: Strap on the Belt of Truth

Monday: Make-fast the Breastplate of Righteousness

Tuesday: Tread in the Shoes of Peace

Wednesday: Wield the Shield of Faith

Thursday: Think within the Helmet of Salvation

Friday: Fight with the Sword of the Spirit

Saturday: Steadfastly Pray in the Spirit

This pattern has enabled me to pray more effectively for myself, my loved ones, and others throughout the world by focusing on a different piece of God's armor each day of the week. This has helped tremendously. I can be driving in my car, sitting at my desk or out jogging and feel the need to pray.

My first thought is, "Okay, what day of the week is it? Well, it is *Sunday*, so we need to *strap* on the Belt of Truth." I then begin to pray on the armor of God. I pray for God's truthfulness in my own life, I pray for God to fill my wife with his truth, and I pray for my kids to desire truth and to love truth. I pray for my friends to be filled with God's truth, for our church to be a place of truth, and for our nation to return to truth. Finally, I pray for the whole world to be filled with an awareness of God's truth. Wow—what a great way to pray!

Or, if it is Monday, I pray, "God, please *make-fast* the Breastplate of Righteousness." *Make-fast* is an old fashioned phrase that means "to fasten" or "to put on." I continue on this course every day of the week and thereby pray the armor of God in a systematic and enjoyable way. Every day of the week we can pray for the ones we love.

We can put each piece of God's armor on ourselves and on those we love—through prayer! By praying the armor of God, we learn how to pray with power and successfully fight against the forces of evil.

If you'd like to learn to pray the armor of God, the best method, I believe, is by doing, not just reading. So take a moment, focus your thoughts, and pray the following prayer out loud:

Lord,
> I want to learn to put on your full armor through prayer,
> > and I want my loved ones to do the same.
> Teach me, through your Word,
> > how to pray on the armor of God
> > for myself and for those I love.
> In Jesus' name, Amen.

Now, I know some of you didn't do this. You read the prayer silently to yourself, but didn't stop to focus on God, to *pray* the prayer, and pray it out loud. It is extremely important to vocalize our prayers, as we will learn together in Chapter Six. For now, please shift into reverse for a moment. Go back, actually focus on God and pray the prayer out loud. Then, I encourage you to do this every time we reach a prayer in this book. *Pause, focus* on communicating with God, and pray each prayer *out loud.* Trust me, in time this will produce rich rewards in prayer. Pray the prayer aloud as an authentic request from you to your heavenly Father. Now shift into forward, and we can proceed.

Living in a Battle Zone

Before we begin learning to pray each piece of armor, we might first ask the question, "Why do we need armor, anyway?" The simple answer is *because we are in the midst of a dangerous spiritual battlefield, with arrows flying all around us.* There is a spiritual war going on around us and without adequate armor, we certainly will be severely wounded.

Christians, though, often forget this. One woman in our

church, for instance, called me recently quite distraught. She was a pastor's daughter, her husband a fine Christian man, and they had always raised their children to love the Lord and go to church. She was shocked and mortified to discover that her teenage son was experimenting with drugs. "How could this happen?" she exclaimed. "He knows we think this is terribly wrong."

A part of my prayerful response to her was, "Well, you have an enemy who is trying to destroy you and your family and tear you all down. If he can attack one of your kids, he will. You and your family are in a battle zone, and a bullet from the enemy has hit your son."

She replied, "But I thought as Christians we were protected from Satan's attacks! I never thought this could happen to us. What do I do now?"

Every church leader and pastor has received calls like this. The evidence is compelling: we are living in a battle zone. Spiritual warfare is very real.

Skeptics in the Battle Zone

Skeptics, though, may doubt the reality of this spiritual warfare. If you or someone you love is a skeptic, the answer to "Why do we need armor?" can't start with, "Well, the answer is spiritual warfare." Instead, in Socratic fashion, allow me to answer sincere skeptics with a series of questions that force us to take a look at some things that most of us don't like thinking about, which lie painfully just beneath the surface of our daily lives:

Why is everyday life so difficult?

Why is it so hard, in our culture, to remain married...or even moral?

Why is it so hard to keep our promises...to withstand temptations...to control our anger...to not become mired in materialism?

Why is it so difficult for Christians to behave like Christ?

Why does life sometimes seem to be an almost endless series of struggles?

Why can't we fix our own lives?

You see, the very same people who are skeptical of spiritual matters probably will not doubt that life is a very difficult struggle for all of us. But why is this so?

Why is life on earth so difficult? The answer can be found in 1 John 5:19. Talking about Christians, John says, "We know that we are children of God, and that the whole world is under the control of the evil one." That's the problem, and the surprising source of our struggles: *the whole world is under the control of the evil one!* We have enemies—Satan and his cohorts— and they are out to destroy us. In other words, *we are at war*, and have been all our lives. According to the Bible, this war has been going on not only our whole lives, but at least since the creation of the world. The enemy has been shooting his weapons and flaming arrows at God and at us. This is why life seems to be such a struggle.

"But wait," a skeptic might protest. "I don't believe in the existence of God or supernatural beings. I don't believe I am in a battle zone." Well, just because the skeptic doesn't believe in something, it does not necessarily follow that the skeptic is right. It could be that the skeptic is simply unaware or is willfully blind to such matters. It may take a hit by a spiritual arrow or perhaps a spear to convince the skeptic otherwise (it just depends on the thickness of one's skin and defenses).

For instance, a few years ago I received a call from a friend of mine who I've known since the seventh grade. He was not a Christian and had been skeptical of Christianity for years, even after his wife became a believer. Though we had gone to the same junior high and high schools, and played on the same football team, our worlds grew vastly apart. Two decades later, his wife began attending the church in which I serve. Suddenly, he began attending church with her and their kids.

So why did he call me? Well, he was in trouble: he had been wrongly accused of a serious crime. It was a classic case of an innocent person being in the wrong place at the wrong time but, nonetheless, he was going to be arrested and maybe put on trial. He said to me, "I can't believe this is happening to me. I'm a good man! A good husband and father. I don't deserve this."

I said, "You're right. You are a good man and no, you don't deserve it. But I've been trying to tell you that God exists, and so does real evil—Satan. The truth is that you have an enemy who wants to mess up your life and your family's life—you have an enemy who is out to destroy you. I believe that all of us are living in a spiritual battlefield. We are living in a combat zone, with arrows flying all around us, but you keep trying to pretend that there are no arrows and no enemy. Well, now you've really been unfairly hit. You are on the front line."

He said, "That's just what it feels like right now!" We went on to discuss his situation, and talked about how important it was to have a great attorney to defend him. This struck me as an evangelistic opportunity, so I asked, "Do you think it's really important to have a good attorney on your side when you stand before the judge? Would you ever stand before a judge alone, without an attorney?"

"Absolutely not," he replied. "There's no way I'd want to stand before a judge alone."

After a short pause, I said, "Well, this is just what I've been trying to tell you: some day you are going to die and you will stand before the ultimate judge of all—God—and you will be guilty and all alone. But Christians will have Jesus, God's Son, standing beside them as their advocate, their defense attorney, so to speak. Now do you understand why you need a Savior? He quietly said, "Wow! That makes a lot of sense to me now." Less than a week later, he surrendered his life to Christ.

The Bible's shocking answer to the age-old questions, "Why do bad things happen?" and "Why can't we fix our own lives?" is singular and simple: the cause of the problem is not merely within us. The problem is an ancient enemy outside us. Life is difficult because we have a hostile enemy who is warring against us.

In Ephesians 6:10-12, the Apostle Paul describes the reality of this hostile enemy:

Finally, be strong in the Lord and in his mighty power. Put on the full armor of God so that you can take your stand against the devil's schemes. For our struggle is not against flesh and blood, but against the rulers, against the authorities, against the powers of this dark world and against the spiritual forces of evil in the heavenly realms.

In other words, life is difficult because we have an incredibly difficult, highly organized, and darkly devious enemy.

Unfortunately, many people today are completely unaware they are involved in daily warfare with an evil enemy. They are in the middle of a combat zone, with casualties and injuries all around them, yet they somehow remain completely ignorant of the reality and hostility of the enemy.

Imagine what would happen to a real army if this were the case. What if a squad of soldiers on the battlefield did not realize that they were at war? Instead, they assumed their problems were just the result of conflict within their own unit. Of course, they might have internal conflict too, but the real danger is from the outside enemy. The stark reality is that many problems in life—in our marriages, families, cities, states, and countries—are *primarily* the result of spiritual warfare, and, only secondarily, the result of internal conflict.

This is one reason I am intellectually attracted to Christianity. I find attractive the Judeo-Christian ethic as revealed in the Bible because the Bible doesn't suggest that life is a picnic. There is no implication that life gets easier if you work harder, think smarter, or try to get along better. The Bible is honest about the fact that there is a real evil in our world; and we cannot fix, change or ignore that reality.

Once we grasp this, the sensible question is, "Well, what can we do against this enemy?" Fortunately, after Paul explains this reality he tells us how we can then protect ourselves from this evil:

> Therefore put on the full armor of God, so that when the day of evil comes, you may be able to stand your ground, and after you have done everything, to stand. Stand firm then, with the belt of truth buckled around your waist, with the breastplate of righteousness in place, and with your feet fitted with the readiness that comes from the gospel of peace. In addition to all this, take up the shield of faith, with which you can extinguish all the flaming arrows of the evil one. Take the helmet of salvation and the sword of the Spirit, which is the Word of God. And pray in the Spirit on all occasions with all kinds of prayers and requests. With this in mind, be alert and always keep on praying for all the saints.
>
> (Ephesians 6:13-18)

Evil is real. Dark, evil forces are warring against us. Therefore, we must learn how to fight against these formidable foes. We must learn how to arm and use the protection and weapons God has placed at our disposal, which Paul calls "the full armor of God." This is why we need armor—we are in the midst of a battle!

Before we move ahead, let's pause again for a moment of prayer. Please pray the following prayer out loud to your loving Lord.

> Lord,
> I sincerely desire that both myself and my loved ones
> could put on the full armor of God through prayer.
> But Lord, I have enemies who don't want this to happen.
> They want us to remain vulnerable and unprotected.
> Now that I realize this,
> I pray even more urgently and fervently,

please put your armor on me and my loved ones.
In Jesus' name, Amen.

Are we strong enough to fight this enemy?

How can we protect ourselves from the evil one? Are we strong enough to fight against this vicious enemy? Remember what Paul said to the Christians at Ephesus: "Finally, be strong in the Lord and in his mighty power. Put on the full armor of God so that you can take your stand against the devil's schemes." Then three verses later Paul repeats, "Put on the full armor of God" (Ephesians 6:10, 13).

As we have just discussed, the problem is that we are at war. The solution is to grasp that we are not strong enough to fight against this vicious foe alone. If we try to fight with our own strength and protect ourselves with our own human armor, we will fail miserably. In fact, that's exactly what most of us are doing. That is why Paul begins by emphasizing that in order to wage this war, we must do it in the strength and power of the Lord, and we must be armed with his armaments and not merely our own.

Just to drive this home, let's try a little exercise. Pray these next sentences aloud to the Lord:

Lord,
I am not strong enough to fight the evil one.
If I try to fight him with my own strength,
I will fail miserably.
In Jesus' name, Amen.

Pray it again…and then a third time!

This is why it is so crucial that we learn to *pray* the armor of

God. To be completely honest, it has taken me many years of Christian living—and failing repeatedly—to learn this. In the past I was always taught the armor of God by an expository and didactic analysis of what each quality in the pieces of armor represented. Then, I was encouraged to *try really hard to be those things.*

For instance, I was taught about the biblical notion of truth, I was then directed to *try* to live that way. The image of the belt of truth as the armor *of God* melted away, and I was then instructed to *try* to speak truthfully, to *try* to act truthfully, and to *try* to live truthfully. I was supposed to *try* to hang out with truthful friends, and *try* to challenge dishonest people to realize the error of their ways. In a way, I was unwittingly *trying to create a piece of armor for myself*—the armor of truth. It was my job to be truthful, which is to say that the armor would be as strong as I was able to make it.

But that was precisely the problem. I wasn't strong enough to make my own armor, and neither are you. None of us can fight successfully with our own power. Remember, Paul said we are to "be strong in the Lord and in his mighty power." Truthfully (pun intended), I can't trust myself to be completely truthful—even with myself. So a belt of my own design and making isn't going to be sufficient. I don't merely need my belt of truth around me; I need *the Lord's* belt of truth. It's an admirable goal to try to be truthful, but God's belt is infinitely stronger.

Let's try that little prayer again. Pray the following statement out loud:

> Lord,
>   I am not strong enough to fight the evil one.

> If I try to fight him with my own strength,
>   I will fail miserably.
> And if I try to arm myself against him,
>   I will also fail completely.
> Give me wisdom for how to put on your armor, Lord.
> In Jesus' name, Amen.

What then can we do? Instead of trying to live truthfully or put on our own belt of truth, the better solution, dear fellow-struggler, is to faithfully and forcefully pray the armor of God.

The full armor of God

Furthermore, we fight as soldiers of God by putting on the *full* armor of God. Paul said, "Put on the full armor of God," not just a few pieces. Some Christians misunderstand this concept. They think that all they need is to be saved, which in this passage is to wear the helmet of salvation. They believe (maybe unconsciously), "Oh, I'm saved, so I don't need anything else." But there is a problem here. If Christians just have on the helmet of salvation, then their heads are protected but the rest of them is open to warfare. They are vulnerable to attack. Other Christians may feel that because they are persons of peace (i.e. they have the shoes of peace on) they are protected. But they also leave the rest of their body and soul vulnerable to attack. If we want to protect ourselves and our loved ones, we need to pray on the *full* armor of God.

How does the armor of God work?

We must really concentrate here and look closely at the text.

26

Notice that, in Ephesians 6:10-18, Paul's instructions on how to defend ourselves against evil have *nothing to do with evil.* In my opinion, this is where some books on spiritual warfare go astray from the biblical text. They try to fight against evil by concentrating on the different schemes and ploys of the enemy. Instead, the biblical way to engage in warfare and fight the darkness is *not to concentrate on the darkness.* We fight the enemy by focusing on the Lord.

Look at verse 10. Paul doesn't say to be strong in deliverance tactics, in exorcism prayers, or in our understanding of evil. Instead, he says "...be strong in the Lord and his mighty power." In other words, the way we defeat evil and darkness is by focusing on Jesus, who is also known as the light of the world.

Of course, we already know this in the natural world; it is just common sense. When we are home late at night and go into to a dark room, how do we get rid of the darkness? Do we look at the dark, study the darkness, and speak against the darkness? Do we yell in a loud voice, "Darkness, be gone!" or "Darkness, I rebuke thee!" Of course not. In order to get rid of the darkness in our home *we turn on the light.* It is the same way in the supernatural realm. To get rid of the darkness we turn on the light of Christ. We bring Jesus into the situation, which is to ask him to fill us and by his very presence shine the light of glory. Light always conquers darkness. Light always prevails. Jesus said, "I am the light of the world," (John 8:12) and the Bible says that God himself is light (1 John 1:5). This is how we fight darkness successfully.

Sadly, I know several Christians who have made terrible mistakes in this area. I know of one Christian leader who concentrated too much on evil and on darkness. He focused on exorcisms and deliverance, and spent much time studying these dark themes. This focus, though well-intentioned, had a corrosive, deleterious effect on him, and his life began to unravel. He tried to battle evil by focusing on the ways of evil. No—that is not the Ephesians 6 battle plan at all.

Who do we think we are anyway? Strong enough to fight the devil or his demons? No way! If we try to do that, we will surely be defeated. Instead, the way to fight evil is not to focus on evil but, instead, focus on the Lord. We concentrate not on the darkness, but on the light. We arm ourselves and protect ourselves by putting on Christ, as Paul says: "Clothe yourselves with the Lord Jesus Christ." (Romans 13:14)

What this all comes down to

In my own training as a follower of the Lord, I have come to experience the greatest degree of protection and power through the simple combination of these two biblical/theological concepts:

1) Praying the armor of God

2) It is light that dispels darkness

As followers and soldiers of the light, we fight best by clothing ourselves with the very character and person of Christ, and then by allowing the light of Jesus to shine in and through us.

Where do we go from here?

We now have a plan to pray on the armor of God daily. We

understand that the armor of God isn't something we clothe ourselves in through our own effort. Rather, we appreciate Christians can only put on the armor of God through prayer, and we realize the way to overcome darkness is to turn on the light. So where do we go from here?

In the rest of this book, we will discuss how to put each element of the armor of God on ourselves and on those we love—through prayer. This will teach us how to pray with power and successfully fight against the forces of evil. Each chapter will cover a specific piece of armor and explain in detail how to pray each day to protect ourselves and others against evil. When we focus on praying to God, we learn how to turn on the light of God in our lives. This dispels the darkness of evil from our lives one day at a time.

But before we plunge ahead, let's take a moment to pause and pray. Remember our little prayers to the Lord in this chapter? Let's pray the same words out loud again, but this time as a complete, heartfelt prayer to God, finishing by praying Ephesians 6:10:

> Lord,
>> I am not strong enough to fight the evil one.
>> If I try to fight him with my own strength,
>>> I will fail completely.
>> And if I try to arm myself against him,
>>> I will fail miserably.
>> Instead, I ask you to strengthen me, Lord,
>>> with your mighty power.
>> I ask you to put on me the very character of Christ,
>>> because it's light that overcomes the darkness.
>> I ask you to put on me your full armor, O God,

so I can take my stand against the devil's schemes.
In Jesus' name, Amen.

I suggest that you use this simple prayer, or some variation of it, to begin your daily time of *Praying the Armor of God.* In my own life, I pray some form of this introductory prayer for myself, and then I pray on the specific piece of armor for that day (as we will see in ensuing chapters.)

Next, I always pray for my wife. I pray some variation of this prayer for her, by name:

Lord,
>   My wife, Amy, is also not strong enough
>   to fight the evil one.
>   If she tries to fight him with her own strength,
>   she will fail miserably.
>   And if she tries to arm herself against him,
>   she will fail completely.
>   Instead, I ask you to strengthen her, Lord,
>   with your mighty power.
>   I ask you to put on her the very character of Christ
>   because it's light that overcomes the darkness.
>   I ask you to put on her your full armor, O God,
>   so that she can take her stand
>   against the devil's schemes.
>   In Jesus' name, Amen.

Give this a try right now. Pray the preceding prayer aloud, but substitute the name of a person of significance in your life. For instance, begin the prayer with, "Lord, I pray for my boyfriend, Alex…" or "Lord, I pray for my neighbor, Karen…"

After this introductory prayer, I also pray the specific armor of the day for my wife. Next, I pray for my three children, one by one, in the same way. I then continue on with my parents, my siblings, extended family, and close family friends. Then, I do the same for my co-workers, our church body, our community, our government, our nation, and finally our world. It takes some time to do this, but once you get the hang of it, it all flows smoothly and naturally. I then finish my prayer time with other specific requests.

How to protect those you love

On the day my youngest son, Jesse, told me that his English class TA was stoned, I knew that a great way to protect him was to continue to keep the lines of conversation open, to keep talking about these things. and to keep encouraging him. I also knew that I needed to monitor his new friendships and keep an eye out for any slippage. But as I drove home, I found myself praying silently for him, even as we continued to talk and drive. I prayed a silent prayer of thanks— and then several intense prayers of protection:

> Lord,
> Please continue to protect my son from evil forces.
> Please continue to keep his heart turned towards you.
> Please help him not desire or give into
> the many temptations at his high school,
> but keep him pure and clear and sober-minded.
> Give him wisdom beyond his years.
> Please help him be a light to these kids who need you
> and your love so desperately.
> In Jesus' name, Amen.

Then I naturally and easily began to pray the armor of God upon him.

Silently, I prayed:

> Lord,
>> My son, Jesse, is also not strong enough
>>> to fight the evil one.
>> If he tries to fight him with his own strength,
>>> he will fail miserably.
>> And if he tries to arm himself against him,
>>> he will fail completely.
>> Instead, I ask you to strengthen him, Lord,
>>> with your mighty power.
>> I ask you to put on him the very character of Christ,
>>> because it's light that overcomes the darkness.
>> I ask you to put on him your full armor, O God,
>>> so that he can take his stand
>>> against the devil's schemes.
>> In Jesus' name, Amen.

After I was done praying, I felt great! I can't really explain it, but I knew:

- I've spent quality time with the Lord.

- I've prayed in a biblical, effective and simple manner.

- I've been armed and empowered to face that day's battles.

- I've benefited those I've prayed for through the grace and power of God, and have asked God to arm and protect them.

- I'm ready to look to God this very day to answer these prayers.

Chapter Two

Sunday: Strap On the Belt of Truth

"One word of truth outweighs the whole world."
— *Alexander Solzhenitsyn*

It's time to start learning specifically how to pray on the armor of God and what each piece of armor represents. It is only fitting that we start this chapter as we ended the previous: in fervent prayer. The repetition is purposeful. As we gradually memorize this prayer each day when we begin to pray the armor of God, our prayer life will strengthen and our prayer vocabulary will increase. Please pray this prayer aloud right now:

Lord,
> I am not strong enough to fight the evil one.
> If I try to fight him on my own strength,
>> I will fail miserably.
> And if I try to arm myself against him,
>> I will fail completely.
> Instead, I ask you to strengthen me, Lord,
>> with your mighty power.
> I ask you to put on me the very character of Christ,
>> because it's light that overcomes the darkness.

I ask you to put on me the full armor of God,
  so I can take my stand against the devil's schemes.
In Jesus' name, Amen.

As we begin to protect our loved ones from evil by praying the armor of God each day of the week, we learn the first piece of armor God directs us to put on is the belt of truth. Paul said in Ephesians 6:14, "Stand firm then, with the belt of truth buckled around your waist." But how do we do this? How do we pray on the belt of truth? How will this help protect ourselves and our loved ones from the influence of evil? How can truth help us overcome common struggles that we all face in life? And why is "truth" the first spiritual weapon for which we are taught to pray?

In order to answer these questions, we first should take a long look at ourselves and our culture and ask why truth is so rare in the first place. In other words, why is it so difficult to be people of truth? Let me say this a more personal way: why is it so hard to not tell lies, to not stretch the truth, to not fib a little? We humans seem to be inveterate liars—we even lie to ourselves. What's wrong with us?

Strapping on the belt of truth is both especially difficult and desperately important due to the amount of untruth in our culture. Our culture today neither values truth nor even believes in the reality of truth. In fact, our culture is so darkly deceitful, that we should immediately pray for help and for the light of God's truth to shine in minds and hearts of us all. This is impossible to overemphasize: it is so difficult not to be self-deceived. I might even hazard to suggest that on this side of Glory, everyone will be, to some extent, self-deceived. As Paul wrote to the church in Corinth:

Now we see but a poor reflection as in a mirror;
then we shall see face to face. Now I know in part;
then I shall know fully, even as I am fully known.

(1 Corinthians 13:12)

Yes, we must continually remain humble about our grasp of truth, even open to instruction and growth in our understanding of God's ways and his Word. We need to continually remind ourselves that we don't want our own truth, but we want God's truth, no matter how painful or difficult it is to accept.

Please pray this prayer out loud:

Lord Jesus, help me!
    I am in the middle of a war,
        and the enemy is attacking me from all sides.
    I am unable to be a person of truth without you.
    I am unable to discover truth without you.
    I am unable even to be honest with myself without you.
    So I ask you, shine your light upon me now,
        open the eyes of my heart to your truth.
    I pray this in the name of Jesus, Amen.

We pray on the belt of truth

We probably wouldn't have guessed this on our own—that the very first piece of armor, the very first thing to protect us from evil, is the belt of truth.

Is this the first piece of armor you would choose if you were already on a battlefield with incoming spiritual arrows? Because the attacks were underway, I think I would probably pick up a shield first to protect myself. Or maybe I would first put on a breastplate to protect my heart or a helmet for my head. But God teaches us here, in

35

Ephesians 6:14, that the belt of truth is our primary and first weapon.

Historically, a soldier's belt was not technically a piece of armor, but instead, a normal and essential piece of clothing. For both Greek and Roman soldiers, their full armor was called *panoply* (which literally meant a full set of armor, since it is derived from the Greek term *pan*, meaning full or all, and *hoopla*, meaning armor or a suit of armor). What were the collective pieces that made up a soldier's panoply? Wilbur Fields provides a good summary in his commentary on the book of Ephesians:

> The Romans copied their armor from the Greeks, but changed it considerably during the centuries. The Greeks used bronze for their armor, but the Romans used more iron. The Greeks showed their artistic nature in the design of their armor. Roman armor was less beautiful, but more practical.
>
> The historian Polybius (about 200 B.C.) wrote a description of Roman armor in his time. Polybius said that the Roman panoply consisted, in the first place, of a shield (*thureos*), and that along with the shield was a sword (*machaira*). Then next came two javelins (*hussoi*), a helmet (*perikephalaia*) and a greave (*knemis*). The majority, when they had further put on a bronze plate, measuring a span every way, which they wore on their breasts, and called a heart guard (*kardiophulax*), were completely armed. But those citizens who were assessed at more than 10,000 drachmae wore instead, together with the other arms, cuirasses made of chain mail.[1]

You have probably noticed the first piece of armor mentioned

---

1   Wilbur Fields, The Glorious Church (Joplin, MI: College Press, 1960), p. 189.

by Paul, the belt, was not mentioned in Polybius's list of armor. Strictly speaking, a belt was not a piece of armor but simply an essential piece of clothing—not just for soldiers, but also for everyday citizens. It was not like the belts worn by police officers today, full of devices and holders for various weapons. Nor was it, in a comic book sense, like the famous "Bat-belt," which Batman always had at his fingertips for any crime-stopping or life-saving device needed. As a kid, I thought it was funny that Batman always had on his belt precisely the tool he needed. Even at a young age it was clear to me there was no way a single belt could accommodate every tool I had seen Batman use at one time or another. Anyway, the point here is the belt of truth Paul references is a far cry from a military belt, an ammo holster, or a Bat-belt.

Instead, Paul is referring to the simple belt nearly all adults wore, even the poor who often used a piece of rope. A belt was necessary due to the fact that common people did not have "tailored" or "fitted" clothes ("Tailor" comes from a Latin root, *taliare*, which meant "to cut", because tailored clothes were cut to closely fit the measurements of a particular person). Of course, this is such the norm today that it is difficult for us to imagine a time when there were no stores in which ready-made clothing could be purchased. But the ancient world knew nothing of fitted pants and shirts: these are fairly modern conveniences. In the time of Jesus and Paul (indeed—for most of recorded history), clothing typically was made by immediate family members.

In biblical times, most people wore simple tunics, sometimes both an inner and outer tunic, depending on the weather. A tunic was a single, rectangular piece of cloth, folded and sometimes roughly sewn on two sides, with holes cut for one's head and arms. Tunics would fall naturally along one's torso and down to the lower legs or feet. Because tunics were not fitted, they would be cumbersome to walk or work in, especially when fighting. For this reason, a belt was strapped around one's waist, to keep the flowing garment under control.[2]

If a person needed to run or fight, the lower portion of the tunic would be raised up and tucked under the belt, a process that was called "girding the loins." In fact, the word "gird" (from which is derived the term "girdle") means to encircle or bind something with a flexible band. This is just what the belt did for the tunic. It encircled and bound the loose and flowing parts of the tunic to the soldier's body so he could fight less encumbered, or it allowed a non-soldier to run or work vigorously.

When Moses was instructed how to eat the Passover meal in order to leave Egypt, God said, "This is how you are to eat it: with your cloak tucked into your belt, your sandals on your feet and your staff in your hand. Eat it in haste; it is the Lord's Passover" (Exodus 12:11). They were to eat in readiness to flee, symbolized by, as the King James Version translated this passage, their "girded loins."

In the same way, we believers are instructed by Jesus to be ready for his return by being "dressed ready for service" (Luke 12:35), which literally reads in the King James Version, "let your loins be girded about." Peter also uses the same expression concerning the

---

2 Jeremiah used a simple linen belt as a moving metaphor for God's protective love: "'For as a belt is bound around a man's waist, so I bound the whole house of Israel and the whole house of Judah to me,' declares the Lord, 'to be my people for my renown and praise and honor. But they have not listened.'" (Jeremiah 13:11)

believer's mental readiness (1 Peter 1:13).

In all of these cases, the point of girding a belt around one's waist is to prepare and ready oneself. Therefore, to have "the belt of truth buckled about your waist" (Ephesians 6:14) simply means "get ready for action." And how do we get ready for action? It's with a sure grasp and possession of the "truth."

So, the first insight we can apply in praying on the belt of truth is that a military belt signifies our understanding that a struggle is just ahead of us, and we are preparing and readying ourselves for the fight. We can pray like this:

> Lord,
> I'm on a battlefield and facing a long and difficult struggle.
> Help me not be caught unprepared,
> but instead help me be ready
> and fully prepared for battle.
> In Jesus' name, Amen.

Why is the belt the belt of "truth"?

Now we have arrived at the point where we can answer the question: why is the first item of armor *truth*? Why aren't we told to put on the belt of peace or the belt of salvation?

The answer is that "truth" is a fundamental perspective on reality that enables us to correctly add the additional pieces of armor. We put on truth first because we live in a world of deception, and we must first have truth in order to identify the other pieces of armor correctly.

Without truth, how can we be sure that the breastplate of righteousness is really God's concept of righteousness and not some mistaken version of righteousness foisted on us by our culture?

Without truth, how can we be sure any piece of armor is truly God's version: His view of peace? His understanding of faith? His definition of righteousness, etc.? Yes, before we can, with full assurance, put on any other piece of armor, we first must solidly pray on God's truth. Only then can each ensuing piece of armor be correct.

So what is "truth"? Even Pilate famously asked Jesus, "What is truth?" (John 18:38), the very question philosophers have struggled with for thousands of years. It's hard for me to not go off on a tangent here, because I have a deep interest in philosophy and the history of ideas, so I will simply summarize and then briefly explain my own definition of truth: *Truth is the awareness that reality is actual and exclusive.*

First, truth is the awareness that reality is actual. To believe that truth exists is to believe that the facts of existence are as they are, independent of me. As the popular saying goes, "It is what it is." Truths concern objective reality, not merely my perceptions of reality. If reality is actual, then there are "true-truths" (as Francis Schaeffer used to phrase this[3]), truths that are true simply because that is the way existence actually is. For instance, water is made up of two parts hydrogen and one part oxygen because that is the actual chemical reality of the substance we call water. The molecular make-up of water does not depend on our opinions or perspective.

In like manner, Christians believe that God has created *real* things: matter, energy, laws, beings, and even informational sequences. These things actually exist; that is, there is a truth to their essence and make-up. Things are what they actually are, not what we'd like to

---

3   Francis Schaeffer, *Escape from Reason* (Downer's Grove, IL: IVP, 1968), p. 29.

think or to choose them to be.

The problem is that we live in a world that believes truth is relative and we can rename or redefine things according to our own desires; we can *spin* the truth to serve our own purposes. But when we claim that there is such a thing as truth, we are saying that reality and real beings cannot be changed by merely changing descriptions—which is what spin essentially does.

For instance, God either exists or he doesn't; our different opinions about God do not change his essential reality. Another example is Jesus himself: Jesus either is the only way to God or he is not; He is either the universal Savior or he is not. Other world religions may appreciate the historical Jesus and may try to include him in their theological system (such as Islam or Mormonism) so they try to redefine him and make him into something other than who he claimed to be. Take Islam, for example: Islam teaches Jesus was one of the prophets, he did not die on the cross (since God would never allow one of his prophets to die in such a manner), and there was no resurrection. The facts of the matter speak otherwise: Jesus differentiated himself from the other prophets (Matthew 16:13-20), and both the crucifixion and resurrection of Jesus are well-attested events of history. Just calling something by a different name does not change its actual reality.

An anecdote involving President Lincoln illustrates the fact that we can't change something just by renaming it. As the story goes, Lincoln was talking to a man one day, and they argued back and forth for some time. Try as he might, Lincoln just couldn't convince this man about the truth of the matter. Finally, Lincoln grasped the nature of this disagreement and then said, "I think I understand the problem. Let me ask you two questions to illustrate. First of all, can you tell me how many legs a cow has?" And the man, in a demeaning tone, said, "Well, of course, a cow has four legs." Lincoln replied, "Correct. But now suppose we call the cow's tail a leg. Now how many legs does the cow have?" The man thought for a moment and said, "Well, it now has five legs." Lincoln replied, "No, you are wrong. Just because you call a tail a leg, doesn't mean the cow has more legs. It still has only four legs no matter what you call it." Lincoln knew that truth was a matter of facts and not merely a matter of opinion or nomenclature.

In the same way, truth is truth no matter what we call it. But in today's world, spin is everything. Today, many of us think we can change the definitions of whatever we want because there is no truth and all is opinion. No! Truth is truth. It doesn't matter that we agree that it is the truth.

Why is this so important? The existence of actual truth concerning every real thing will enable us to grasp the *truth* about righteousness, the *truth* about salvation, the *truth* about peace, etc. For example, righteousness is not defined in any way we choose; there is a truth about righteousness that is as it is in God's created design. To put this in a different way: truth is not relative. So, to gird our loins with truth is to prepare ourselves for action by seeing things as God sees and designed them.[4]

Let's pause for a moment and turn to God in prayer:

---

4 Christians realize that knowing God's truth also will require faith, which we will discuss in Chapter Five. In fact, just as to be fully protected we need all the pieces of armor, so too we need truth, faith, God's Word, etc., to have full knowledge.

Lord,
>I pray for your truth to fill my mind.
>But Lord, I live in a world of untruth where
>>lying is the norm.
>I am often confused by so much that is said
>>in the media, by politicians,
>and even by Christian leaders that disagree.
>Help me, Lord.
>I want to see reality as you see it;
>>I want to know your truths
>>and be able to discern right and wrong,
>>good and evil as you do.
>In Jesus' name, Amen.

Dishonesty is now the norm

In the book *The Day America Told the Truth*[5], people were asked, "How often do you lie and to whom do you lie?" Here are some of the amazing results:

1) People were asked, "How many of you lie about important matters?" The results are shocking, but not surprising:

- 36% lie about important matters. (That means that out of three people you know, one of them may have lied to you about something very important. How does that make you feel about your family, friends or neighbors?)

2) What about honesty in marriages? Is it any better between husbands and wives? Spouses were asked: "How many of you regularly lie to your spouse?" The startling result was:

- 69% lie to spouses. (No wonder so many marriages fall

---

5 James Patterson and Peter Kim, *The Day America Told the Truth* (New York: Prentice Hall Press, 1991).

apart—they are filled with deception! This means that two-thirds of all married individuals have been significantly deceived in some way by their spouses.)

3) Does truth fare any better with families? How about honesty among siblings, friends, and children?

- 73% lie to siblings.
- 75% lie to friends.
- 86% lie regularly to parents. (It used to be that parents taught their kids that honesty is the best policy. It is now the case that families are filled with dishonesty).

4) Finally, 91% of those surveyed lie routinely about matters they consider trivial. Let's think about this for a moment. Someone who routinely lies is what we might call a habitual, a compulsive, or a regular liar. In a culture where lying is the regular thing to do, it is the honest person who becomes abnormal. No wonder no one trusts what anyone does or says in politics, the news professions, or the media today. They don't even trust each other. What a disaster.

What is the shocking conclusion we must draw? It is just this: Most of what we hear in our culture is untrue. (I'm sure my skeptical readers may now be asking: "How about you, Rick? Doesn't this mean that you are lying too?" The answer is: no. Just because much of what we hear is false, it does not follow that everything we hear is a lie.)

Yes, many of the things we see, hear, or read in modern culture are lies. As Mark D. Roberts mentions in his book, *Dare to Be True*, there is pervasiveness to deception in America today. One study noted that of 2.6 million job applications, 44% contained "not just minor exaggerations but out-right lies." A survey of teenagers found that 92% admitted lying to their parents in the last year. 78% admitted lying to their teachers. Deception is also pervasive in the medical profession: Roberts quotes Dr. Robert Burten who says concerning medical professionals, "Lying is everywhere."

Roberts also cites a study by Robert Feldman of the University of Massachusetts, who found lies fill normal conversation. In a series of case studies, Feldman placed complete strangers together and had them carry on a conversation for ten minutes. The shocking result? Sixty percent of these people later admitted to one lie in that ten minute conversation, and over 50% lied more than twice! Feldman concluded, "People tell a considerable number of lies in everyday conversation. It was a very surprising result. We didn't expect lying to be such a common part of life."[6]

How can this be? Is it really possible that in everyday, casual conversations, over 50% of the population routinely lie? How did we ever get in such a mess?

What a mess!

Readers of the Bible will quickly recognize this is not a recent phenomenon. The Bible is refreshingly honest about deception— even the lies of its heroes. (This is another aspect I love about the Bible: it doesn't sugarcoat its characters, but reveals them, warts and all.) Right at the start, Adam and Eve were taken in by lies and tried to excuse their way out of trouble. Their son Cain followed suit and lied to God about the whereabouts of his brother Abel, giving the famous

---

6   Mark D. Roberts, *Dare to Be True* (Colorado Springs, CO: Waterbrook Press, 2003), p 4.

excuse, "Am I my brother's keeper?" (Genesis 4:9) Abraham lied to Abimelech, king of Gerar, by saying his wife, Sarah, was just his sister (Genesis 20:2). His son Isaac was a chip off the old block, and said the same about his wife Rebekah (Genesis 26:7). Then, Isaac and Rebekah's son Jacob deceived Isaac into giving him the older son's blessing (Genesis 27:1-29).

In fact, the very name "Jacob" means "one who grasps the heel," which in Hebrew figuratively means, "he deceives." Throughout the Bible, the lying continues: Samson deceived Delilah (Judges 16:4-22), David prevaricated to the king of Gath and feigned insanity (1 Samuel 21:13), and Israel slowly became a nation of liars (see Hosea 10:1-4). The lying continued into the New Testament when Judas lied to Jesus, saying "Surely not I [will betray you], Rabbi?" (Matthew 26:25). The nadir of deception occurs when Peter, the Rock and the leader of the disciples, lied three times just before the crucifixion of Jesus. (Luke 22:54-62)

As the Bible so clearly reveals, deception and lies are indeed everywhere. Why is this so? The Bible's answer is very clear, found in Jesus' charge to the religious leaders of his day:

> You belong to your father, the devil, and you must carry out your father's desire. He was a murderer from the beginning, not holding to the truth, for there is no truth in him. When he lies, he speaks his native language, for he is a liar and the father of lies. Yet because I tell the truth, you do not believe me!
>
> (John 8:44-45)

According to Jesus, our enemy, the devil, is "a liar," "the father of lies," and "there is no truth in him." In an age when two-thirds of spouses lie to each other and over 90% of Americans as a whole lie routinely, let's not forget that Satan lies *100%* of the time. There is *no* truth in him.

When we add his position of power to this proclivity towards deception, the result is a potent, and in some cases, a deadly combination. Satan is described by Jesus as "the prince of this world" (John 12:31; 14:30; 16:11) and by Paul as "the god of this age" (2 Corinthians 4:4). As the ruler of this world who lies continually, it should come as no surprise that people in this world are confused and deceived. Paul puts it this way in 2 Corinthians 4:4a: "The god of this age has blinded the minds of unbelievers."

Yes, the Bible claims that the devil has "blinded the minds" of non-Christians. Their ability to understand and to think correctly has been compromised and corrupted, their propensity toward perversity is increased; their thinking is askew and twisted. To use another biblical metaphor, their minds are "darkened." And what is the remedy for darkened minds? Of course, just as we discussed in Chapter One, the solution for darkness is not to focus on the darkness, but to turn on the light. For this reason the complete text of 2 Corinthians 4:4-6 reads:

> The god of this age has blinded the minds of unbelievers, so that they cannot see the light of the gospel of the glory of Christ, who is the image of God. For we do not preach ourselves, but Jesus Christ as Lord, and ourselves as your servants for Jesus' sake. For God, who said, "Let light shine out of darkness," made his light shine in our hearts to give us the light of the knowledge of the glory of God in the face of Christ.

Furthermore, since darkness is what happens when light is

47

removed, the Bible describes the end of Satan as a condemnation to complete and utter darkness (Revelation 16:10). This makes complete sense because if "God is light; in him there is no darkness at all" (1 John 1:5), then to be absolutely cast from the presence of God is to be cast into absolute darkness. Jude describes fallen angels as now being "kept in darkness" and fallen humans will be those "for whom blackest darkness has been reserved forever" (Jude 6, 13). Let's take this thought to God in prayer:

> Lord,
>> I'm starting to get it;
>>> the light is dawning in my heart and mind.
>> I can see now that our world is so messed up,
>>> confused, and hurtful.
>> Because the god of this world,
>>> the father of lies and hatred and hurt,
>>> has blinded the minds of those who do not
>>> yet know your Son, the light of the world.
>> Lord, I pray for those I love,
>>> take the blindfolds off their minds.
>> I pray for those I live by and work with,
>>> take the blindfolds off their hearts.
>> I pray for those around the world and especially
>>> for leaders, take the blindfolds off their eyes.
>> Help us all to see you, your truth, and bring
>>> your light and hope to a world in darkness.
>> In Jesus' name, Amen.

This is why it's so important to put on the belt of truth. When we lie, we give the devil a foothold. For me, this has been a revolutionary insight. In the past I thought a lie was just an innocuous choice: I could choose to lie just as I could choose what kind of dessert

I wanted—chocolate or vanilla. But lying is no minor matter; speaking and living the truth is a part of spiritual warfare. This is why Paul said to the Christians in Ephesus, "Do not give the devil a foothold" (Ephesians 4:27). I came to realize, as a result of praying the armor of God, that when we lie in attitude, thought or behavior, we willingly open our lives to the devil and give him a foothold. Satan attacks and attaches himself to those who deceive. When we lie, we take off the belt of truth. We remove an essential part of our spiritual armor. Then (*zing*) here come the fiery darts of the wicked one — right into our lives, right into our families, ready to kill and destroy. How could this have happened? What left us so unprotected? This is the deceit of deception: the evil one whispers that lying won't hurt us, but, in truth, it doubly hurts us. It is our fault because we opened ourselves up; we took off the belt of truth voluntarily.

The solution to darkness

Fortunately, into our world of deep and deceptive darkness, Jesus came to shine the true light of God. Jesus said about himself, "I am the way and the truth and the life" (John 14:6). Jesus also said, "I am the light of the world. Whoever follows me will never walk in darkness, but will have the light of life" (John 8:12). Jesus is the truth and so we fight against evil by not focusing on evil. We don't try to defeat Satan, because that would be focusing on darkness. Instead, we turn on the light, and live in the light. We turn on the light and truth of Jesus. He is the ultimate truth. We protect ourselves by putting on the first piece of the armor of God, the belt of truth, which is to say that we put on Jesus himself. Matthew describes Jesus as the fulfillment of the prophecy of Isaiah:

> The people living in darkness
> > have seen a great light;
> on those living in the land of the shadow of death
> > a light has dawned.
> > > (Matthew 4:16; Isaiah 9:2)

As a result, followers of Jesus are called "children of the light." Paul stressed this point to the church in Ephesus:

> For you were once darkness, but now you are light in the Lord. Live as children of light (for the fruit of the light consists in all goodness, righteousness and truth) and find out what pleases the Lord. Have nothing to do with the fruitless deeds of darkness, but rather expose them. For it is shameful even to mention what the disobedient do in secret. But everything exposed by the light becomes visible, for it is light that makes everything visible. This is why it is said:
>
> > "Wake up, O sleeper,
> > > rise from the dead,
> > and Christ will shine on you."
> > > (Ephesians 5:8-14)

So Christians are "children of the light" who "live in the light," because Jesus is the light of the world. When the light of God is shining, truth is clear and self-evident. When the darkness of evil prevails, it is difficult to see truth. That's why Paul earlier told the Ephesians to not be blown about by "every wind and teaching and by the cunning and craftiness of men in their deceitful scheming." Instead, he reminded them that speaking the truth brings about desirable results:

> Speaking the truth in love, we will in all things grow up into him, who is the Head, that is, Christ.
> (Ephesians 4:14-15)

Yes—light leads to truth and honesty. When light shines, when truth and honesty are upheld, love blossoms. Deception leads to death and misery, darkness and destruction. In contrast, truth leads to love, joy and new life. Paul continued to teach the Ephesians,

> Therefore each of you must put off falsehood and speak truthfully to his neighbor, for we are all members of one body. "In your anger do not sin." Do not let the sun go down while you are still angry, and do not give the devil a foothold. He who has been stealing must steal no longer, but must work, doing something useful with his own hands, that he may have something to share with those in need.
> (Ephesians 4:25-28)

In other words, true thinking will lead to true living, and our actions will begin to bring health and wholeness to our families, our community and our world.

Let's get practical

Up to this point, we have claimed that truth is not relative. Instead, truth is the way things actually are in God's created design. Truth is a description of what things are in reality. We have also seen that we live in a culture of deception where truth is a rare commodity. Our study about the armor of God, so far, has been fairly theoretical; it's time now to get practical.

What is truth on a practical level? The belt of truth is the ability to speak and live honest lives in line with what God intended us to be. It is a commitment that we are going to be honest individuals, regardless of what people around us do. It doesn't matter how embarrassing the situation or how profitable the lie; truth must prevail. We are going to be men and women of truth. We are going to buckle this belt around us and pray for God's truth to shine in and through us. In a world that does not believe in truth and is enveloped in dishonesty and darkness, we are going to stand firm and live lives of honesty and light.

Honesty really is the best policy. That's why we need proactively to pray on the belt of truth. We commit ourselves to truth, and the light will cause the darkness of falsehood to disappear. "Therefore, each of you must put off falsehood and speak truthfully to his neighbor, for we are all members of one body" (Ephesians 4:25). When we do this—speak truthfully with ourselves and with one another—a delightful, secondary consequence follows: we begin to *live* truthfully. In Ephesians 4:26 Paul goes on to say, "In your anger do not sin and do not let the sun go down when you are still angry." Truthfulness will affect how we behave towards others. Anger often escalates due to a lack of honesty. Furthermore, the abundant gifts God has provided to each of us were not meant for the self alone, but for those who are in need. Paul explained, "He who has been stealing must steal no longer, but must work, doing something useful with his own hands, that he may have something to share with those in need" (Ephesians 4:28).

So, truth in speech results in truth in action. If we steal, we are pretending that something is ours, and that's not the honest truth. Truth affects how we live, it affects love relationships, it affects our self-control and it affects our lifestyle. Truth has powerful consequences. Truth is one of the strongest weapons we have to fight evil; it is one of the most potent arms in the Christian's arsenal.

Truth is a strong weapon

The greatest leaders of our 20th century understood this. For example, Winston Churchill took over as Prime Minister when Great Britain was at its brink of disaster. Churchill's predecessor, Neville Chamberlain, had effectively surrendered the continent to Hitler through appeasement, and it seemed his own country soon would be swallowed also. In the face of the huge Nazi war machine, which was taking over Europe, Churchill knew that Great Britain had only one weapon left. What weapon was strong enough to still beat Nazi Germany? Truth. Winston Churchill faced the truth, spoke the truth, and used truth to help defeat Nazi Germany. For instance, Churchill said to the House of Commons, after taking office as Prime Minister on May 13, 1940:

> I would say to the House, as I said to those who have joined this Government: 'I have nothing to offer but blood, toil, tears, and sweat.' We have before us an ordeal of the most grievous kind. We have before us many, many long months of struggle and suffering. You ask, what is our policy? I can say: It is to wage war, by sea, land and air, with all our might and with all the strength that God can give us: to wage war against a monstrous tyranny, never surpassed in the dark, lamentable catalogue of human crime. That is our policy. You ask, what is our aim? I can answer in one

53

word: It is victory, victory at all costs, victory in spite of all terror, victory, however long and hard the road may be; for without victory, there is no survival.

No spin—just truth. Then, on June 4, 1940, he said to the House of Commons:

We shall go on to the end, we shall fight in France, we shall fight on the seas and oceans, we shall fight with growing confidence and growing strength in the air, *we shall defend our Island, whatever the cost may be, we shall fight on the beaches, we shall fight on the landing grounds, we shall fight in the fields and in the streets, we shall fight in the hills; we shall never surrender*, and even if, which I do not for a moment believe, this Island or a large part of it were subjugated and starving, then our Empire beyond the seas, armed and guarded by the British Fleet, would carry on the struggle, until, in God's good time, the New World, with all its power and might, steps forth to the rescue and the liberation of the Old.

No sugarcoating—just truth. Then on June 18, 1940 he said to the same House:

Upon this battle depends the survival of Christian civilization. Upon it depends our own British life and the long continuity of our institutions and our Empire. The whole fury and might of the enemy must very soon be turned on us now. Hitler knows that he will have to break us in this Island or lose the war. If we can stand up to him, all Europe may be free and the life of the world may move forward into broad, sunlit uplands.

But if we fail, then the whole world, including the United States, including all that we have known and cared for, will sink into the abyss of a new Dark Age, made more sinister, and perhaps more protracted, by the lights of perverted science. Let us therefore brace ourselves to our duties, and so bear ourselves that, if the British Empire and its Commonwealth last for a thousand years, men will still say, "This was their finest hour."

No soft-pedaling—just truth!

Alexander Solzhenitsyn, a dissident in Communist Russia during the Cold War of the 1960s and 1970s, knew the same thing. The Soviet Union was at its strongest when he began to write, and he knew from personal experience that communism was full of wickedness and was an immensely diabolical scheme. But how could he overcome Soviet Russia? He was only a solitary writer. He then realized that he had in his possession the strongest weapon, in fact, the *only* weapon that was able to overcome Communist Russia. What was his weapon? Truth. In a famous address to Harvard he said, "One word of truth outweighs the whole world." His statement, at the time, seemed little more than wishful thinking. But time and truth marched on, and the Soviet Union was formally dissolved on December 25, 1991.

An American, Mark Helprin, expressed a similar thought. As a *Wall Street Journal* writer, Helprin was recently asked about the dangers and problems in our world and what America could do to combat evil. He said, "America has the greatest weapon on our side. Truth is the consummate weapon."

Like Churchill, Solzhenitsyn, and Helprin, Christians have a weapon at our disposal that is able to overcome darkness and despair, a weapon that is able to protect ourselves and our loved ones from evil. We have the consummate weapon. It is truth. The only question is, will we use it?

How to protect those we love

To sum this all up: *Honesty is a powerful weapon against evil.*

Do you want to protect your kids from evil? Do you want to guard your marriage from harm? Do you want to protect your friends from darkness? Would you like to protect your church? Your community? Your country? Your world? You've got the weapon. You just need to ask God to strap the belt of truth on you and start using it. How often should we pray about this? I have found, in my personal prayer life, that praying this one day a week—and more often when needed—works wonders. The first day of each week, of course, is Sunday, so we can use the "**S**" in Sunday to remind us to "**S**trap on the belt of truth." In this way, once a week, we remind ourselves to pray for God to put his belt of truth on ourselves and those we love in order to protect us all from the enemy who seeks to gain a foothold in our lives.

Do this on a regular basis and see what happens. Every Sunday, I like to pray for God's truth in my own life and in my marriage. As a father, I especially like to pray that my kids might be committed to truth and repelled and disgusted by deception. I pray that our church can become more and more a place of truth, and I pray the same for our community, our nation, and our world.

Do you think our world would be a better place if more people were praying for truth? What do you think would happen to marriages if, every

Sunday, all spouses prayed for honesty and for God's truth to prevail in their union? What would happen if our church leaders, our business owners, and our politicians were to pray this regularly?

What the world needs first is truth. God's truth. So pray on the first piece of the armor of God, the belt of truth. Don't just do this every once in awhile; pray for it on a regular, weekly basis. Pray on the armor of God and you will be amazed—and eternally grateful—for the changes that happen.

Let's end with a prayer for this very thing:

Lord,
    I'm on a battlefield
        facing a dark and deceitful enemy,
    Please put on me the belt of truth.
    May I see through the lies of this world.
    May I grasp the truths of your Word.
    May I put off falsehood and speak only truth.
    May I be able to discern right from wrong,
        good from evil, light from darkness.
    And may Jesus, the Truth and the Light,
        live in and through me.
    In his name, Amen.

Chapter Three

Monday: Make Fast the Breastplate of Righteousness

"Monday Monday, can't trust that day…"

So sang The Mamas & The Papas in 1966, and the song became an instant and enduring hit. It expressed exactly how most people feel on Mondays. The song went on to say,

> Every other day, every other day,
> Every other day of the week is fine, yeah
> But whenever Monday comes,
>   but whenever Monday comes
> You can find me cryin' all of the time…

For most people, Monday is a tough day. It's the day we end our weekend of rest, worship, and time with family, and mope off to work singing the I-have-to-go-back-to-work blues. Some folks hate it so much that, for them, Monday is a not just a loathsome day, it is the most difficult day of the week.

But why can't we trust Mondays? For Christians, each Monday is a prime opportunity to be reminded that there is an enemy lurking and ready to deceive us, an opponent who would lead us, and those we love, away from God and the goodness he has for our lives. The song says we can't trust Mondays, but there is someone who is worse, whom we definitely cannot trust. Who or what is this untrustworthy scoundrel?

Surprise! It is not our boss, not our coworkers, not the non-Christians at the office who tempt us in sundry ways, and not just the Prince of Darkness himself. The enemy is more subtle and less-often noticed. It is inside us. Our enemy, according to the Bible, is our own heart.

How to pray on Mondays

The Apostle Paul instructs us, in Ephesians 6, to put on the armor of God to protect ourselves and those we love in the battle against evil. In order to win the battle, the key is to realize that success will not be achieved through our own efforts to be better and more godly people. Instead, the crucial point is this: the true and complete armor is the armor *of God*, and thus each piece is something only God can fasten on us. We cannot put it on ourselves. Since we are so easily self-deceived, as we learned in the last chapter concerning truth, we will never win the war against falsehood just by trying harder to be truthful. Thus we prayed, on Sunday, for God to do this in our lives and the lives of our loved ones, which is to say we prayed for God to strap on us his belt of truth.

This is true every day of the week. Because we cannot put the armor of God on ourselves, we need to come before God in prayer each day, confessing that we are unable to protect ourselves from the evil one, and asking for God's help with one piece of armor per day.

59

Yesterday, we confessed and then prayed for God to arm us with the belt of truth. Even though today is a new day, so we begin with the same confession that we used yesterday, and will use each day:

Please pray this prayer aloud right now:

Lord,
    I am not strong enough
        to fight the evil one.
    If I try to fight him on my own strength,
        I will fail miserably.
    And if I try to arm myself against him,
        I will fail completely.
    Instead, I ask you to strengthen me, Lord,
        with your mighty power.
    I ask you to put on me the very character of Christ,
        because it's light that overcomes the darkness.
    I ask you to put on me the full armor of God,
        so that I can take my stand against the devil's schemes.
    In Jesus' name, Amen.

After we have the belt of truth secure, the next piece of armor we don for protection is the breastplate of righteousness. Why is this important? Shouldn't we put on the helmet of salvation next? Or the shield of faith? What's so important about righteousness?

The first truth to grasp about righteousness

In order to answer this question, first of all it is important to recognize a fundamental truth (which we are capable of doing since we learned, in the last chapter, how to strap on the belt of truth). The fundamental truth is this: we live in a world devoid of righteousness, filled with cultures that are twisted and immoral. Our society is terribly messed-up, and when we add together the other messed-up societies on our planet, that inevitably produces a messed-up world. The Bible says the whole world is under the control of the evil one, which somewhat explains our predicament (1 John 5:19). Our world is unrighteous because it is controlled by the instigator and father of unrighteousness.

To be sure, this has always been the case¬ since the fall in the garden—yet some cultures seem to be especially good at unrighteousness (maybe that should read "bad at righteousness"). Some cultures are especially vile and wicked, whereas in other cultures, for a time, righteousness seems to blossom. In America, for instance, there have been seasons of cultural improvements in righteousness, such as after the great revivals of the 18th and 19th centuries, and also during or immediately after the cessation of devastating wars, such as the Civil War and World War II (this is because the horrors of war often cause people to clean up their spiritual acts, albeit temporarily).

Our downward unrighteous spiral became clear in two surveys that were taken of American public school teachers, one in 1940 and the second in 1990. In both cases, the teachers were asked, "What are the greatest problems you as teachers face?" Here were their answers:

<u>1940</u>

    Talking out of turn

    Chewing gum

    Making noise

    Running in the halls

Cutting in line

Dress code infractions

Littering

1990

Drug abuse

Alcohol abuse

Pregnancy

Suicide

Rape

Robbery

Assault

Wow, the American culture has certainly changed in the last 50 years. We might even conclude that our world has become so immoral and blinded by evil, that people can't even see the difference anymore. People are so used to darkness, that they now think it's normal. Fifty years ago, Americans had a clear sense of right and wrong: it was right to be married and sexually faithful to one's spouse; it was wrong to be sexually active outside marriage. Now, of course, it is more common for people to be sexually active before marriage, and it is uncommon for young people to marry as virgins. Fifty years ago, it was right to stay married and it was wrong to divorce; today divorce is common and couples that remain married for 40 or 50 years are the oddities. Fifty years ago, companies were loyal to their employees and vice versa; today loyalty is considered as passé as the dinosaurs. Fifty years ago, abortion was wrong and Down Syndrome babies were cherished as "special." Today such babies are identified *in utero* and are aborted as unfit to live.

Yikes! Our culture is so steeped in unrighteousness that we need to take this to God in prayer (remember, pray aloud):

> Lord,
>> Our culture is broken and twisted,
>>> obviously and firmly under the control of the evil one.
>> Marital faithfulness is out and divorce is in,
>>> commitment is passé and cohabitation is en vogue.
>> Abortion is considered an inviolable right,
>>> while praying in public is considered offensive.
>> Dear Lord, lying and deceit are now the norms
>>> whereas people of honesty are the exceptions.
>> Even our TV shows, during the evening family hour,
>>> are full of foul language, vivid violence, and naked sexuality.
> We are lost—lost and bereft of any sense of your righteousness,
> and we cannot find our way back.
> I beg you to put on us the breastplate of righteousness,
>> so that we can take our stand against the devil's schemes.
> In Jesus' name, Amen.

How have we drifted so far from God's righteousness? The answer is both simple and subtle: it is because the prevailing morality of our society is *do your own thing.* Beginning in the late 19th century with the publication of Darwin's *The Origin of the Species*, our western culture abandoned the notion of God as creator and designer of all. Though there were some philosophers who abandoned belief in God before Darwin, *The Origin of the Species* opened the door for scientists, academics, and finally the common people to also do away with the premise that a creator and designer necessarily exists.

63

This led our society to jettison the idea that there is a moral lawgiver in heaven—God—who has predetermined what is right and what is wrong. Instead, we abrogated that right to ourselves, deciding that moral decisions are best left up to the individual. If we want to divorce our spouses, we no longer need a rationale to do so. If we want to abort our babies, it's perfectly legal. If we prefer to marry a person of our same gender—or if we want to change our gender—well, that's okay too. Anything goes!

A sad and telling example is found in the book *The Day America Told the Truth*[7] , which recorded the answer people gave when asked, "What would you do for ten million dollars?" Ten million dollars is a lot of money, and according to this book, two-thirds of the people surveyed said they would do one of the following actions in order to be $10,000,000 richer:

- 25% said they would abandon their entire family.
- 25% would abandon their church.
- 23% would become prostitutes for a week or more.
- 16% would give up their American citizenships.
- 16% would leave their spouses.
- 10% would withhold testimony and let a murderer go free.
- 7% would kill a stranger.
- 3% would put their children up for adoption.

These statistics are so shocking—so chilling—that one might mistakenly conclude that one-fourth of the people in our country are real losers, people who are morally handicapped. But that would be to underestimate the survey results. As I mentioned before listing

---

7   Patterson and Kim, *op. cit.*

each action, *two-thirds of the people surveyed said they would agree to do one of these things.* You may feel this survey does not represent what two-thirds of the people in your family or church would do, but it must represent some folks somewhere, people in our schools, neighborhoods, places of business, and yes, even in our churches. Sit back and cogitate on this fact: two-thirds of the people in your city would do one of these things. If you live in a community of 100,000 people, there are not 23 that would prostitute themselves if the price were right—there are 23,000. In like manner, there are 25,000 who would abandon their families, and 7,000 who would kill a stranger for money. 7,000! This means that even in a small town of only 10,000 people, there still are 700 who would kill a stranger for money.

This is why it is so important for us to focus on the breastplate of righteousness. Our world is completely riddled with evil and enslaved in darkness due to the absence of righteousness.

Let's pause and pray about this:

Lord,
    We are aghast at the moral depravity
        that surrounds us today.
    We live among people that would not only sell themselves
        for the right price (becoming prostitutes!),
        but they would sell out their spouse, their kids,
        their church and their country.
    Good God, many would even kill for money.
    Please, Dear God, we pray that you protect us
        and our loved ones from this world of wickedness.
    We pray you put on us your breastplate of righteousness.
    In Jesus' name, Amen

The second truth to grasp about righteousness

Though the statistics are shocking, the overall conclusion we have just drawn is probably no surprise to you: our world today is a very unrighteous place. But why is our world so unrighteous? Is it the fault of the Darwinists? Is it due to a broken educational system? Is it the poor example that Hollywood stars provide? Or can we blame it on the politicians, like we do everything else? While all of these are contributing factors, the real blame belongs closer to home.

This is the second fundamental truth, which is imperative to grasp today: our country—indeed, all cultures—are twisted and immoral because they are filled with creatures who are likewise twisted and immoral. Let me put it bluntly: we are all mess-ups, which inevitably produces our messed-up societies and messed-up world. The Bible says that, except for Jesus himself, there never has been a perfectly righteous person (1 Peter 2:22; Romans 3:10). That includes you and me. All cultures are fallen from God's Edenic intention because all humans have fallen from our original garden perfection.

We Christians must admit that even we are an unrighteous lot. Some Christians wrongly assume that they arc not unrighteous because they don't kill, steal, or commit adultery. As the saying went, they "don't smoke, drink, chew, or go with girls who do."

But the truth is that we all are exceedingly unrighteous. Churches are full of people who are prideful, who gossip, and who are judgmental. We hold grudges, we are greedy, and we are gluttons (full disclosure: those three are a few of my many sins; what are yours?). Like the Apostle Paul, we do the very things we do not want to do, and *vice versa* (Romans 7:14-24). For instance (as we faced in the last

66

chapter), we desire to be honest people and live with uncompromising integrity, yet every one of us, more often than we would like to admit, veers from the truth.

We tell white lies to avoid hurting others: "Yes, I think your new hairstyle is great" or "No, those pants don't make your hips look big." We exaggerate facts or experiences: "The fish I caught was *thiiiiis* big" or "Our church attendance is *thiiiiis* large." Or, we keep silent instead of speaking the truth in love, such as speaking out on today's moral issues. And our failures in speech are just one subset, one area among many in the larger scope of unrighteousness, in which we fall regularly. Let's take this matter to God in prayer.

> Lord,
> Now I get it: our society is broken
>   because I am broken.
> I am broken and twisted,
>   and am myself firmly under the control of the evil one.
> I do the very things I do not wish to do,
>   and I do not do the things I wish to do.
> I often speak before thinking,
>   and also often fail to speak up when I should.
> I criticize others for their unrighteous behavior,
>   but seldom confess
>   the depths of my own unrighteousness.
> My thought life is sometimes filled with notions
>   that I would be embarrassed if others knew.
> If heaven is a perfect place,
>   then I am clearly disqualified,
>   even though others consider me to be
>   a pretty good person.
> I now see clearly
>   that being a good person is not good enough.

I need you to forgive me,
   to wash me as white as snow,
   to remember my sins no more,
   to cleanse me of all unrighteousness.
In other words, I need a Savior.
I ask Jesus Christ to be my Lord and Savior.
I commit the rest of my life to him and his service.
I ask you to place on me the breastplate of righteousness,
   so that I can take my stand against the devil's schemes.
In Jesus' name, Amen.

The only way to become righteous

In other words, the only way to become righteous is to ask the Righteous One, Jesus Christ, into our hearts and allow him to take residence as Lord and Savior. The Bible is very clear—we cannot become righteous on our own volition. The prophet Isaiah said that "all our righteous acts are like filthy rags" (Isaiah 64:6). The Apostle Paul wrote the church in Galatia, "If righteousness could be gained through the law, Christ died for nothing," (Galatians 2:21) and he told the Philippian believers his desire was to "be found in him, not having a righteousness of my own that comes from the law, but that which is through faith in Christ—the righteousness that comes from God and is by faith" (Philippians 3:9). He made a similar statement to the church in Corinth: "God made him who had no sin to be sin for us, so that in him we might become the righteousness of God" (2 Corinthians 5:21).

Isn't being a 'pretty good person' good enough?

Of course, our culture completely misunderstands this. Most Americans blithely assume that they will go to heaven when they die, if there is such a place, because they are 'pretty good' persons. But heaven, the Bible teaches, is a perfect place that "nothing impure will ever enter" (Revelation 21:27). 'Pure,' of course, means perfect, not 'pretty good' or 'better than others.' Plus, the verse is awfully clear in its limitations: *nothing* impure will *ever* enter. So 'pretty good' is not good enough.

Furthermore, what would happen to heaven if God were to allow one 'pretty good' person in, followed by another and so forth? Sooner or later, conflicts would arise, and we would have the same hellish experience that we have here on earth. We would ruin heaven. No, the entrance requirement for heaven is not a 'pretty good' resume: it is a flawless, spotless, righteous, perfect life. Who besides Jesus would qualify? No one, including you and me.

Essentially, we can neither save ourselves nor make ourselves righteous. This is why we must pray for God to put the breastplate of righteousness on us, rather than try to do so ourselves. We simply cannot be righteous on our own, no matter how hard we try.

As a new Christian, I learned this the hard way when I assumed it was my job to be righteous. I assumed it was my sole duty to put this piece of armor, the breastplate of righteousness, on myself. I remember this clearly: I'd try to be righteous, try to be holy, and try to go a day without sin. But I just couldn't do it. When I did seem to have a good day, I found myself feeling prideful about it, which ruined my goodness for the day.[8] I was a failure either way. Putting the breastplate of righteousness on myself never worked for me, just

---

8 Benjamin Franklin experienced the same difficulty. When he was successful at the first 12 of his virtues, he worried he would be so prideful that he could never succeed in the 13th virtue: humility. Benjamin Franklin, *Autobiography* (Philadelphia: Henry Altemus, 1895), p. 162.

as it didn't for King David, or the Apostle Paul, or anyone else in the Bible except for Jesus.

We cannot put the breastplate of righteousness on ourselves, but we can ask the Lord Jesus, the Messiah, to do this for us, since he has done this successfully for himself:

> Justice is far from us,
>> and righteousness does not reach us...
>
> The Lord looked and was displeased
>> that there was no justice.
>
> He saw that there was no one,
>> he was appalled that there was no one to intervene;
>> so his own arm worked salvation for him,
>> and his own righteousness sustained him.
>
> He put righteousness on as a breastplate,
>> and the helmet of salvation on his head...
>>> (Isaiah 59:9,15-17)

Yes, once again the armor of God is not something we can place on ourselves, like we dress ourselves with clothes. The armor of God is *his armor*, not ours, so only God himself can handle its pieces and dress us with it. Isaiah himself experienced this and said, switching metaphors slightly,

> "I delight greatly in the Lord;
>> My soul rejoices in my God.
>
> For he has clothed me with the garments of salvation
>> and arrayed me in a robe of righteousness..."
>>> (Isaiah 61:10)

The book of Revelation depicts this when, after the triumphant return of Christ, those "who had been slain... each were given a white robe…" signifying, of course, the complete and utter righteousness that can only be received as a gift of God, and never something that we can earn or deserve (Revelation 6:9, 11). In fact, the number of those who are made righteous in this way is countless:

> After this I looked and there before me was a great multitude that no one could count, from every nation, tribe, people and language, standing before the throne and in front of the Lamb. They were wearing white robes and were holding palm branches in their hands…"
>
> (Revelation 7:9)

Dear reader, if you have never taken the opportunity to ask Jesus Christ into your heart as Lord and Savior, do it now. Read aloud the prayer on pages 59-60 again, and then tell others of your new decision to follow Jesus. Find a church, be baptized and get involved. This is the only way to make fast the breastplate of righteousness—we must ask Jesus to do it for us. We cannot save ourselves, we cannot make ourselves holy, and we cannot make ourselves qualified for heaven. Only Jesus can do these things in our lives.

We ask for the same thing that King David requested, "Create in me a clean heart, O God" (Psalm 51:10), and we believe that God will keep the promise he made through the prophet Ezekiel, "I will give you a new heart and put a new spirit in you; I will remove from you your heart of stone and give you a heart of flesh" (Ezekiel 36:26). As a result, we become radically new and different persons, having "his Spirit in our hearts," and "his light shine in our hearts," culminating in a whole new beginning: "If anyone is in Christ he is a new creation; the old has gone, the new has come!" (2 Corinthians 1:22; 4:6; 5:17).

71

Just as "God created the heavens and the earth" in Genesis 1:1, Paul taught the Christians in Corinth that God creates a whole new reality in us. Our hearts are so broken that we don't need just a tune-up, an overhaul, or even an extreme makeover. We need to be new creations.

The third truth to grasp about righteousness

Once we have been made righteous by recognizing and accepting the sacrifice of Christ on the cross (which is to be saved), we can then ask God to help us live righteous lives—at least more righteous than we were able to accomplish on our own (which is to be sanctified). We can ask God to help us live in a manner that pleases him, though we know we will never be able to achieve perfection. We also realize there are benefits to living life as God intended, since Jesus said, "Blessed are those that hunger and thirst for righteousness" (Matthew 5:6). The Bible also says we are to offer our bodies to God as "instruments of righteousness" (Romans 6:13). So how do we do this? How do we, as inveterate sinners, grow in personal righteousness?

Let's call this the third major truth about righteousness: at root, we discover that righteousness is a *heart* issue. The Bible has a lot to say about our hearts, starting with this problem: because of Adam's fall, human hearts naturally gravitate toward evil.

Of course, our culture doesn't understand this. Phrases such as "people are basically good," "all children are pure," and "as innocent as a child," are common. But these simplistic notions are not correct, according to the Bible, which says we are born with a natural inclination to do evil. In Genesis, God talked to Noah, both before and after the flood, about the inbred tendency of humans toward evil. Before the flood,

> The Lord saw how great man's wickedness on the earth had become, and that every inclination of the thoughts of his heart was only evil all the time.
>
> (Genesis 6:5)

After the flood, God's opinion of human righteousness was not much better:

> Never again will I curse the ground because of man, even though every inclination of his heart is evil from childhood.
>
> (Genesis 8:21b)

In both cases, God did not just say that "humans often incline towards evil" or that "some human thoughts turn to evil." Instead, God said *every* inclination of the human heart is always towards evil. In the first instance, the indictment is thrice emphasized: "every," "only," and "all the time." Furthermore, the Bible is clear that it is the human *heart* that is the problem; the source of our trouble is located in our chests. The trouble is not our heads, for as we all know, our heads tend to follow our hearts, and not *vice versa*. In other words, our hearts tend to lead us astray.

What a surprise this is to modern (and postmodern) ears, whose owners glibly assume that they should always "follow their hearts." A friend and I were once talking about this, when he suddenly took off his watch and said, "Rick, look at the inscription on the inside." On the gold-plated, backside cover of his watch, these words were inscribed in flowing, calligraphic script:

73

To my husband on our wedding day. Follow your heart.

Then he said to me,

> This was given to me by my wife on our wedding day. Her advice to me for our marriage was to follow my heart. And guess what? I followed her advice and she is now—as a result—my ex-wife.

He went on to say,

> Rick, written on the back of my watch is the worst piece of advice I ever been given in my whole life. I followed her advice, so when my heart was tempted, I followed my heart. As a result I ended up doing things—bad things—that led to the ruin of our marriage.

That poor, misguided woman. She believed what her culture taught her—that following one's heart was good advice—which she wrote to her groom as her wedding counsel. But in so doing, she sowed the seeds of destruction for her own nascent marriage.

My friend learned the hard way what the prophet Jeremiah taught several millennia ago: "The heart is deceitful above all things and beyond cure. Who can understand it?" (Jeremiah 17:9) Yes, dear friend, this is the key fact about righteousness that our culture misunderstands: we can't trust our own hearts.

Here, I'll prove it to you.

Let's take a survey. How many of you have ever followed your heart and made a big mistake in the process? No—not just a big mistake, but a huge, colossal, *ginormous* mistake. Have you followed your heart and made a big financial purchase that you later deeply regretted? (I have.) Have you obeyed your heart and said something that you later wished you could retract, something that caused you or those you love deep hurt and damage? (I have, many times.) Have you ever listened to your heart and committed a sin that you were later ashamed of and wished you could turn back the hands of time to undo? (I have, countless times.) We all have. I still do, even though I don't want to. At my age I should know better. I buy things I don't need while there are people starving in the world... I say things to my wife that she does not deserve and I later regret... well, enough specifics about me. I'm sure the same is true for you. If we are following our own hearts, we are going to get into trouble. That's why the Bible says, in effect, "Don't trust your heart."

If anyone ever tells you to follow your own heart, tell them, "No, that it is the worst thing a person can do, because our hearts are deceitful and naturally tend towards evil."

Let's pray about this:

Lord,
> I now understand the source of my problems,
>> the reason I keep making poor choices
>> and bad decisions:
>> my heart is a liar!
> My heart is not just deceitful,
>> it is deceitful above all things.
> It tells me to go right when I should turn left,
>> to be silent when I should speak up,
>> to buy or keep when I should give.
> Maybe the wisest way for me to live
>> would be to do the opposite of what my heart suggests,
>> just as it is usually wise to do the opposite

of what the elites of our secular culture recommend.
What can I do?
I can't trust myself and I can't trust my culture!
Lord, I need you to guide me and reveal to me
　　what true righteousness means,
　　and what godly wisdom entails.
Please help me, God.
In Jesus' name, Amen.

How does righteousness relate to a breastplate?

This is why, in the armor of God, the piece that corresponds to righteousness is a *breastplate*. The breastplate, both for Greek and Roman soldiers, was a piece of hammered metal, molded to the rough contours of their chest, and which wrapped around to also cover the back (or, if we believe Hollywood, to represent the pecs and six-pack that lay hidden underneath). Much like today's Kevlar and "bullet-proof" vests, the purpose of a breastplate was to protect the vital organs, especially the heart. In Hebrew, a breastplate was a *shiryown* or *shiryah* (as in Isaiah 59:17 and Jeremiah 46:4; it might have been derived from the Hebrew word to *twist*, as was done to create chain-mail), whereas in Greek it was called a *thorax* (as in Ephesians 6:14 and 1 Thessalonians 5:8). Thorax, as it is commonly used today, is a medical term for the part of the human body situated between the neck and the abdomen, including the collarbones and ribcage, which in turn protects the organs underneath (though when I think of thorax I tend to picture the middle part of an insect's body). Thus, in Greek, *thorax* could refer to the skeletal bones that protect the heart, or the metal armor placed over those bones as further protection for the heart.

This is exactly what we need spiritually. We need spiritual

protection for our spiritual center—which is metaphorically rendered as the heart. So the question becomes, how can we protect our heart from internal error and from external harm?

What can we do? We can't trust our own inclinations or the inclinations of others, even those we love and respect. We can't trust our society, our government, and we certainly can't trust the media.

Fortunately, God has not left us without guidance or instruction. Instead of trusting and following our deceptive hearts, we are supposed to trust what God says to us; we are to trust his Word, which will never fade away (1 Peter 1:24-25). Again, this is an operation that happens not just in our minds, but primarily in our *hearts*. This is why the Psalmist said, "Your word I have stored in my heart, that I may not sin against you" (Psalm 119:11). Notice again, in Proverbs 3:1-4, the importance of following God's advice in our hearts, and the amazing results which follow:

> My son, do not forget my teaching,
>   but keep my commands in your *heart*,
> For they will prolong your life many years
>   and bring you prosperity.
> Let love and faithfulness never leave you;
>   bind them around your neck,
>   write them on the tablet of your *heart*.
> Then you will win favor and a good name
>   in the sight of God and man. (Italics added)

These verses precede two of the most beloved verses in the whole Bible:

> Trust in the Lord with all your *heart*,
>   and lean not on your own understanding;

77

> In all your ways acknowledge him,
>   and he will make your paths straight.
>
> (Proverbs 3:5-6)

It's all about the heart. We can't trust or follow our hearts because our hearts are naturally evil, but we can place God's Word in our hearts. We can do this by reading the Bible regularly, memorizing the Scriptures so they become embedded in our being, and meditating on these passages so they begin to reprogram our heart-inclinations (I'll speak more about meditation in Chapter Six).

This is the ultimate goal to which biblical Christianity aims: a life so saturated with Scripture that our thoughts unconsciously (what I call 'the thoughts of our hearts') shift towards Bible verses during unguarded moments, and our very hearts and lungs seem to keep cadence. What a massive shift this is for most of us who, in our unconscious moments, find our thoughts tending toward worries or past hurts. This is why Paul instructed the Christians in Ephesus,

> Speak to one another with psalms, hymns and spiritual songs. Sing and make music in your heart to the Lord, always giving thanks to God the Father for everything, in the name of our Lord Jesus Christ.
>
> (Ephesians 5:19-20)

I like to think of this heart-music as a radical takeover of the heart, a reprogramming with righteousness, a gradual transformation of the soul. When we memorize and meditate on Scripture, our hearts are changed as we take charge of what is stored in our hearts. We can't achieve righteousness on our own, but we can gain some control over what we allow into our hearts.

It's important what we are storing in our hearts

Jesus taught what we store in our hearts tends to come out later in our thoughts and words. He said,

> No good tree bears bad fruit, nor does a bad tree bear good fruit. Each tree is recognized by its own fruit. People do not pick figs from thorn bushes, or grapes from briers. The good man brings good things out of the good stored up in his heart, and the evil man brings evil things out of the evil stored up in his heart. For out of the overflow of his heart his mouth speaks.
>
> (Luke 6:43-45)

If we want righteousness in our individual lives, if we want our kids to grow up desiring righteousness, and if we want righteousness in our churches, marriages, communities and country, it all depends on what we are storing in our hearts. What have you allowed in your heart? What are you allowing to creep into your kids' hearts? These are important questions because out of the overflow of the heart, we all speak and act.

We have already discussed the importance of storing God's Word in our hearts, along with hymns and spiritual songs. But there is an opposite side to this coin: we must also be careful to not allow evil words, images or thoughts into our hearts. Of course, our culture misunderstands this also, proclaiming, "It doesn't matter what you do in private, as long as you are an adult. It only affects you."

However, a bit of reflection will reveal this is dead wrong. If we allow evil into our hearts, inevitably it's going to come out in our relationships with other people. It is going to mess up others. Many

Christians and non-Christians struggle mightily because they have allowed evil into their hearts, such as addictions to alcohol, drugs, or pornography. These 'private sins' often have devastating family consequences.

My wife spoke with one of our kids about this several years ago. One of our kids was walking with another child, and she could tell from a distance, that they were talking about something they shouldn't be talking about. And so she asked him later on, "What were you talking about?"

Our child said, "Oh, that kid told me a bad joke." Come to find out it wasn't a dirty joke, but it was a morbidly violent joke, which is just as bad.

My wife wisely said, "You know, the problem with listening to a bad joke like that is, once you allow evil into your heart, it is really hard to ever get it out."

For some of us, our hearts have been forgotten and unappreciated for years, left wide open and vulnerable, unprotected. It is time to make fast the breastplate of righteousness. It is time to decide we are not going to let any more evil into our hearts, and instead to ask God to fill our hearts with good—with his goodness. Pray the following out loud,

> Lord, I'm sorry,
>> I've lived all these years as a Christian,
>>> but my heart has been unprotected and undervalued.
>> I haven't worn your breastplate of righteousness.
>>> I've heard things that I should not have heard,
>>> seen things I should have not seen,
>>> and done things I should not have done.

I've let all kinds of junk into my heart,
    while failing to store enough
    of your wisdom and Word there.
Like King David, I need a new heart.
Not just a tune-up or a makeover,
    I need a completely fresh start, a new creation.
I ask you to create a clean, pure heart within me.
Help me store good things in my heart,
    so the overflow of my heart will be
    a blessing to others and an honor to you.
Please put your breastplate of righteousness on me,
    for now and evermore.
In the name of the only Righteous One, Jesus, Amen.

You may have some family members or friends who have strayed from the path of righteousness, and have allowed trash to fill their hearts. Pray the following prayer for them:

God, I'm really worried about these people I love:
    (_____insert names here_____).
They have wandered from your path of righteousness,
    and their hearts have been left unprotected and at risk.
They aren't wearing your breastplate of righteousness.
They've heard things that they should not have heard,
    seen things they should have not seen,
    and done things they should not have done.
They've let all kinds of junk into their hearts,
    while failing to store enough of your love and Word there.
Like King David, they each need a new heart.
    Not just a tune-up or a makeover,
    they need completely fresh starts, to be new creations.
I ask you to create a clean, pure heart within them.
Help them store good things in their hearts,
    so the overflow of their hearts will be

81

a blessing to others and an honor to you.
Please put your breastplate of righteousness on them,
    for now and evermore.
In the name of the only Righteous One, Jesus, Amen.

For your Monday prayer, you might want to pray in this way:

Dear loving heavenly Father,
    I pray on this Monday that you
        make fast the breastplate of righteousness.
    I pray for (_____ insert names of spouse and children _____),
        that you put on them the breastplate of righteousness
        and fill their hearts with your Word and love.
    I pray for (__ insert names of extended family members __),
        that you put on them the breastplate of righteousness
        and guide them today on the paths of righteousness
        for your name's sake.
    I pray for (_ insert names of church members and leaders _),
        that you put on them the breastplate of righteousness
        and protect them from the evil one
        who desires to divide and destroy.
    I pray for (insert names of community and political leaders),
        that you put on them the breastplate of righteousness
        and help them hear your voice
        in a world filled with demonic noise and nonsense.

    I pray for (insert names of international leaders dealing with
        crises around the world),
        that you put on them the breastplate of righteousness
        and that if they do not yet know the love of God in Jesus,
        that you would lead them
        to that all-important discovery.
    May the whole earth be filled with your love,
        your truth, your joy, and your will,
        so that righteousness and peace may kiss together,

and justice may roll down like mighty waters.
I pray this in the name of the King of Righteousness,
Jesus, the only one who is Good, Amen.

Chapter Four

Tuesday: Tread in the Shoes of Peace

Most people today have heard the common saying, "Thank God, it's Friday," but few realize that in the Middle Ages a popular saying was, "Thank God, it's Tuesday." In my book for single adults, I explained why:

> During the Middle Ages, Christian couples were encouraged to abstain from sex on Thursday out of respect for the Lord's Supper (instituted by Jesus on Maundy Thursday), on Friday for the crucifixion, on Saturday to honor the Virgin Mary, on Sunday for the resurrection, and on Monday in memory of departed souls... Their slogan, therefore, became "Thank God, it's Tuesday."[9]

So Tuesday, in medieval times, was a favorite day of the week.

In today's society, Tuesday does not fare as well. For the workers of the world, Monday is a dismal day of recovery, a day to slowly clear out the cobwebs and get up to speed; the weekend is over and it's back to the grind. But then Tuesday hits. The rest and fun of

---

9   Rick Stedman, *Your Single Treasure* (Chicago: Moody Press, 1993, 2003), p. 19.

the previous weekend becomes a faded memory, and yet the coming weekend seems far away, like a distant hope. Tuesday is the day we dig in, put the ax to the grindstone, and do our best at whatever we do to make a living. It's time to go to work in our workplaces, to do our job at our jobs, to hit the books at school.

Since most of us work or go to school on Tuesdays, it also is a good day to consider one's career and the key to success. What is the secret to successful, long-lasting careers? Are successful people smarter, more talented, or do they possess more endurance than the average worker? Are successful people just lucky, fortunate souls who happen along at the right time and the right place? Do successful people have higher IQ's or diplomas from more prestigious colleges? Surprisingly, none of the above factors is the number one predictor of successful careers, according to emotional intelligence expert Daniel Goleman. The number one factor Dr. Goleman claims contributes to workplace success is: one's *relational* ability.[10]

To put it bluntly, many of us—Christians included—don't get along very well with others, and we struggle to maintain long-term relationships. Conflict, in every relationship, sooner or later raises its ugly head and quite often creates large amounts of stress and discomfort. This, in turn, makes life with employers and coworkers miserable, or at least very uncomfortable and unsuccessful. (Of

---

10   In a groundbreaking research paper published in 1973 called "Testing for Competence Rather than Intelligence," David McClelland of Harvard argued, (in Goleman's words), "that traditional academic aptitude, school grades, and advanced credentials simply did not predict how well people would perform on the job or whether they would succeed in life. Instead, he proposed that a set of specific competencies including empathy, self-discipline, and initiative distinguished the most successful from those who were merely good enough to keep their jobs." Goleman summarized the research by saying, "In all the findings, a common core of personal and social abilities has proven to be the key ingredient in people's success: emotional intelligence." Daniel Goleman, *Working with Emotional Intelligence* (New York: Bantam Books, 1988), pp. 16-17.

course, the same is true also in our homes and schools.) Since every relationship will, from time to time, experience friction and conflict, what we need is to become skilled conflict-resolvers, effective relationship-repairpersons. In other words, we need to become peacemakers.

"Breaking up is hard to do"

Now, becoming a peacemaker is much easier said than done. Newlyweds are aware that conflicts will arise in their marriage, and they are confident they will be able to stay in love and maintain the peace—yet most do not. The high divorce rate, and the even higher break-up rate for cohabiting couples, is evidence that maintaining a love-relationship is a hard thing to do.

The same is true in business. In the early years of my ministry, I was excited when two church members decided to go into business together, or when one member was hired by another. But too often I saw conflict ensue, leading to not only the end of the business relationship, but also to the departure of one person or family from our church. Sadly, as a result I no longer feel excitement when church members enter into business together, but instead I feel a sense of dread—and I feel a call to pray extra hard for those relationships.

It seems Neil Sedaka was wrong: breaking up is easy to do. It's staying together that's hard.

Maybe, as our well-intentioned friends advise us, we just need to *try harder*. Try harder to get along with our spouse; put extra effort into our relationship with our coworker; give it the old college try with our neighbor. So we try our best, and yet the relational difficulties remain.

Once again, it has become clear to me, in my own life and in the lives of those I have served in ministry, that the answer is not to just *try harder*. I have seen couples try and try to stay married, only to end up divorced. I have seen parents try and try to reconcile with their kids, only to have the children push them further and further away. And in the one place which should be the most Christ-like and peaceful—the church—I have both seen and personally experienced terrible conflict. I have seen elders become enemies, pastors become opponents, and friends become foes. I write these words with a deep sense of pain, regret, and shame, not pointing the finger of blame at anyone else, because many of these church problems happened on my own watch, and some were occasioned by my own failures. To put it in a nutshell, try as I might, I was not able to keep the peace in our church, and we experienced a hurtful and harmful church schism.

I'm sure the only one happy about it was Satan himself, who seems to be an expert at dividing people. He started right at the beginning, dividing Adam and Eve from God in the Garden. He divided Isaac from Ishmael, Jacob from Esau, and Joseph from his ten older brothers. He divided the Hebrew nation into northern Israel and southern Judea, and he separated the Israelites from the Promised Land when they were taken into captivity in Babylon. The evil one has been at this for millennia, perfecting his craft of creating conflict and division. He is the expert divider, the master of disaster (to quote a line from the *Rocky* movies).

It should come as no surprise that the devil is the great divider because the Greek for demon, *daimon*, comes from the root word which literally means to divide or separate. Our enemy, the devil, uses his demonic forces to separate and divide, with surprising effectiveness. This is why merely trying harder to be persons of peace will never bring success: there is a spiritual war being waged around us, and there are spiritual beings who are working their hardest to divide and conquer. We are not adequate to fight this battle on our own, which is why we need to pray for God to place his armor on us.

Take a moment to pray this prayer aloud, as we are learning to do each day, and as we endeavor to don a new piece of God's Armor:

> Lord,
> I am not strong enough to fight the evil one.
> If I try to fight him on my own strength,
> I will fail miserably.
> And if I try to arm myself against him,
> I will fail completely.
> Instead, I ask you to strengthen me, Lord,
> with your mighty power.
> I ask you to put on me the very character of Christ,
> because it's light that overcomes the darkness.
> I ask you to put on me the full armor of God,
> so that I can take my stand against the devil's schemes.
> In Jesus' name, Amen.

Here is the sober truth: without God's intervention and help, some of your most precious relationships will be broken in the years ahead. Think, for a moment, of your relationships ten or twenty years from now: with which family member will you not be on speaking terms? Which friend will you no longer consider a friend? Will you still be married?

Or think about your kids and grandkids (even if they are in the future for you). Will their marriages survive or end in divorce? Will they have relational success at home, at school, and at work? Will you leave behind a legacy of relational success, longevity, and joy, or will the generations that follow you become more and more fractured?

Think about your relationships at church. Which church leader will turn contrarian and lead an exodus rather than a revival? Which pastor will throw in the towel, give up and resign, rather than deal with disgruntled church folks? Which church friend will become upset about something trivial, will sunder all relationships in your church, and will begin attending a different church in town (training, in the process, their kids to do the same whenever conflict arises)?

Is there something we can do to protect ourselves and our loved ones from these and other relational failures, failures that are so common in our culture? Fortunately, there is something we can do. There is a piece of the armor of God designed just for this; a part of the panoply we can pray for ourselves and others; a spiritual weapon that can help keep our marriages, families, friendships and churches together. What item of armor is that? The day of the week is a reminder: *Tuesday: Tread in the shoes of peace.*

Our goal each day is to learn how to pray with power in this evil world, so that we can protect ourselves and our loved ones from the spiritual forces of darkness at work. On Sunday, we asked God to strap on us the belt of truth. Then, on Monday, we asked him to make fast upon us the breastplate of righteousness. This brings us to Tuesday, the day on which we beseech God to enable us to tread in the shoes of peace. We pray that God put on us the shoes of *shalom*. As the Apostle Paul said in Ephesians 6:15, "...your feet fitted with the readiness that comes from the gospel of peace."

Let's take this to God in prayer:

Lord,
>   I'm so concerned about the high failure rate
>   of relationships in today's culture.
>   I'm worried that someone I love will fail in their marriage,
>   that a person I care about will have trouble with their kids,
>   or a church will experience a demon-inspired split.
>   I'm anxious that some of my kids or grandkids
>   may get divorced
>   or—God forbid—it could even happen to me.
>   God, is there anything I can do?
>   Is there some way I can help families
>   survive the tough times;
>   is there something I can do
>   to help people deal with the problems
>   that inevitably come in every life?
>   Show me, O Lord, according to your word,
>   how I can be a model of peace
>   to my family and friends now,
>   and generationally bless those who will come after me.
>   In Jesus' name, Amen.

A key step in an ancient soldier's preparation

After an ancient soldier secured his tunic around his waist with a belt, and after he made fast his breastplate to protect his heart and other vital organs, the soldier would be wise then, if he had not already done so, to tie on his shoes. The longer one waits to do this task, the more difficult it becomes due to the bulk of the remaining armor.

For a Greek or Roman soldier, shoes were very important, especially if he served in the Mediterranean area. The terrain in the

Middle East was—and still is—very dry and rocky, full of sharp stones. Soft moccasins would quickly tear on the jagged rock edges, and would not provide the support needed to march long distances. Ancient military footwear is sometimes referred to as sandals, but such terminology must not lead us to conclude they wore something like today's flip-flops. Josephus, the Jewish historian, said that the Roman soldiers had footwear that was made of layers of heavy leather, fashioned together and stapled with nails. It was very strong footwear; we might compare it to industrial-quality hiking sandals (such as today's *Keen* or *Teva* brands). In addition, their stiff-soled shoes gave them improved stability and traction. Whereas peasants could walk barefooted and merchants could wear thin-soled shoes, Roman soldiers knew that they were not ready for battle until their feet were fitted with proper shoes.

This is true for military personnel today also. All soldiers know the importance of appropriate footwear. For instance, when American soldiers first went to war in Vietnam, they experienced many problems with their government issued boots. Why? Because the leather boots that had been so workable and serviceable in World War I and World War II simply didn't work in the jungles and swamps of Vietnam. The leather in the boots, when water-logged, quickly fell apart. They discovered that their feet were not well-fitted. The military then invented new boots that were self-draining and self-drying: the GI's (General Infantry) called them "Jungle Boots."

Additionally, both ancient and modern warfare footwear needs to be secured to a soldier's feet before he goes onto a battlefield. When the arrows or bullets are flying around a person, it's the wrong time to bend down and re-tie one's shoelaces. That's why Paul said, "…feet fitted with the *readiness*…"

The same is true, to a lesser degree, in athletics. Shoes are very important for most athletes (with a few understandable exceptions, such as swimmers or most gymnasts). I remember when I was playing high school football, our coach often would say, just before we ran out onto the field to begin the game, "Now men, check your shoes and your shoelaces. Make sure they are tied well, because you don't want to risk losing a touchdown over a loose shoelace."

So we would double-tie and triple-tie our shoes—some of us even taped our shoelaces securely down—because the last thing we wanted was our coach mad at us because we missed a tackle or touchdown if a shoe came off. No experienced athlete gets on the field, hears the starting whistle and says, "Well, I need to put my shoes on now." They put their shoes on before they get on the field. In the same way, as Christians we ask God to put on us his shoes of peace before we enter the battlefield.

The crucial question is: where does the boundary of your battlefield begin? If you are having trouble at work, the preparation time might be as you drive or commute to work. If you are having trouble at church, it might be as you are driving to a church service or meeting. If the trouble is in the neighborhood, it may be as you prepare on Saturday morning to work in the yard. If the trouble is with your kids, it might be before you get out of bed; if it is in your marriage, it might be before you get into bed. If you have trouble in several relationships at once, you may find yourself praying without ceasing.

Let's just take one situation as an example: let's say you are having trouble with a neighbor. As you prepare to go outside to work in the yard or to wash your car, try praying this aloud,

Lord,
    I feel like Noah: I live among the unrighteous.
    I feel like David: I'm facing a giant with a little slingshot.
    I feel like Elijah: I seem to be the only one left serving you.
    But Lord,
        I know you put me in this neighborhood for a reason,
        and I know you put my neighbors here for a purpose too.
    But we have had some conflicts lately,
        unkind deeds were done,
        harsh words were said,
        and hurt feelings were the result.
    Lord, some of my neighbors I don't even want to see,
        others I'd like to give a kick in the pants.
    So I need you to make me a peacemaker.
        I can't do it myself.
    Let me treat others like Jesus would treat them,
        let me forgive them though they may treat me poorly,
        even as Christ forgave those who crucified him.
    Let me speak words seasoned with grace,
        even though they don't deserve them.
    Because you, O Lord, do not treat me like I deserve,
        you give me grace that I have not earned,
        and you speak to me with kindness beyond measure.
    I want to be like you, O Lord, in this neighborhood,
        not like the evil one that others seem to be imitating.
    I'd even ask you to do a miracle of reconciliation,
        since I know that is your specialty.
    Please fill me now with your peace
        that surpasses understanding,

and let your peace flow through me to others.
In Jesus' name, Amen

We can pray a similar prayer, slightly adjusted, during the car ride to a holiday gathering with extended family where conflict commonly occurs, or to a committee meeting with a church member who is upset, etc. Advance preparation is important—and smart. As soldiers check their shoes before battle, so we Christians must also check to make sure we are ready for the relational challenges that will undoubtedly come our way.

The readiness that comes from the gospel of peace

Have confidence when you pray these prayers, because God has already won the battle for us. This is what Paul meant when he said, "...that comes from the gospel of peace." Gospel—or good news—is a literal translation of the Greek word *euaggelion*. The root of the English word *gospel* is: *good* + *spell*, since *spell* also, at one time, meant *tale*, *story*, or *news*. The good news is that Jesus, the Prince of Peace, has come and defeated evil on the cross. He has won for us the victory, and a result of his victory is that we can now be filled with his peace.

Jesus said, "Peace I leave with you, my peace I give to you" (John 14:27) and "I have told you these things so that in me you may have peace. In this world you will have trouble. But take heart! I have overcome the world" (John 16:33).

Think about that statement for a moment: "In me you may have peace." This is either one of the most audacious statements ever uttered, or one of the most awesome truths ever spoken. It is either extreme arrogance, or an all-important truth. Who else could say that but God himself, having come to earth as our Savior and King? This is also why Paul instructs the believers at Philippi,

> Do not be anxious about anything, but in everything, by prayer and petition with thanksgiving, present your requests to God. And the peace of God, which transcends all understanding, will guard your hearts and your minds in Christ Jesus.
>
> (Philippians 4:6-7)

The peace that can guard our hearts and minds, the peace that transcends all understanding, is not a peace we can learn, develop, or achieve. It is "the peace of God." It is God's own peace, coming down upon earth and within the soul of the believer. Here we see again the central theme of this book: the pieces of the armor of God are not items that we have to produce, earn or deserve; instead, they are the very qualities of Jesus himself. Putting on every piece of armor is nothing other than clothing ourselves with, or putting on, Jesus himself. This is why Paul told the Romans, "Put on the Lord Jesus Christ" (Romans 13:14). Jesus is the way, the truth and the life, so putting on the belt of truth is a helpful metaphor for putting on Jesus, who is the truth. Jesus is our righteousness, and when we put on the breastplate of righteousness, that is a symbol for putting on Jesus as our righteousness. Now, as we are instructed to put on the shoes of peace, this essentially means that we are, once again, clothing ourselves with Christ, who is the Prince of Peace (Isaiah 9:6). Clothing ourselves with the armor of God is asking Jesus, and therefore his very

95

character and personality, to saturate and fill our lives. We put on the "armor of light" (Romans 13:12) which Paul clarifies two verses later is tantamount to clothing ourselves with Christ (which makes sense since Jesus is the light of the world).

The bottom line is that we don't have to try to be peaceful (or truthful or whatever). Instead, we need to allow Jesus to live in and through us. We invite him into our lives, give him complete authority, and allow him to live his life through us. As Paul exclaimed, "I no longer live, but Christ lives in me" (Galatians 2:20). In every facet of our being, he fills us with every facet of his being. His truth springs up within us because he is truth, and truth begins to flow out of our innermost being. He pours into us his righteousness, and righteousness begins, of course, to flood from us to others. His peace streams into and then surges through us to satisfy and quench the thirst in others.

Sometimes, we ourselves are surprised by this. We meet a neighbor with whom there is conflict, but we are filled with a peace that surpasses understanding. Rather than the animosity that ruled our hearts in the past, our hearts are filled with the very peace of God as we let Jesus take control and guide our conversations. Now that Jesus is reigning in our hearts, the once dreaded family gathering is transformed as his peace melts old hostilities through kindness and sincere love. Paul's command to the Christians at Colossae "Let the peace of Christ rule in your hearts" (Col. 3:15), becomes a reality rather than just a memory verse. We become peacemakers because the Prince of Peace rules in our lives.

How can I become a peacemaker?

A great goal in life is to be at peace with as many people as possible. Of course, there are both healthy and unhealthy ways to accomplish this. I heard a story of a man who was called for jury duty for a well-publicized murder trial. During the jury selection process, the defense lawyers questioned him intensely:

"Sir, are you a property holder?"

The potential juror responded, "Yes, I am."

The attorney then said, "Are you married or single?"

The man responded, "Married for 20 years."

The final question to him was, "Have you formed or expressed any opinion?"

The man said, "Not for 20 years."

Of course, the courtroom erupted in laughter.

This is, in fact, one way to keep the peace. Live your life without opinions or commitments, and always allow others to have their way. Though this may avoid conflict, it surely is an unhealthy choice for most people.

There is another way to make peace, which Paul expressed in Romans 12:18, "If it is possible, as far as it depends on you, live at peace with everyone." This is a tremendously important insight: peace is not always possible, and sometimes it is not even preferable.

I love the realism of the Bible. Paul did not say that we are expected to live at peace with everyone because, at times, it just isn't feasible. There are people who want to make trouble; there are groups of people that like to run rough over others; there are even political leaders and nations that do this (think of Hitler, Stalin, Pol Pot, Idi

Amin, or Mau Tse-Tung, etc.).

We seek peace "if possible" and therefore when possible. But be careful here: The Bible teaches neither that peace is always the only option, nor that it is always the best option. The Bible does not instruct peace at all costs, or peace in every situation—which is the political philosophy called pacifism. This is an important point because many people in our culture naively assume that pacifism can solve any problem. Sometimes we see protesters on TV, walking up and down the streets or at our universities, carrying placards that say, "No violence," or "Violence is always wrong."

But the Bible doesn't say that violence is always wrong. Frankly, the Bible has a lot of violence in it. As a matter of fact, Jesus "made a whip out of cords" and then turned over the money changers' tables. (So this wasn't just accidental or impulsive violence; this was an act of premeditated violence on the part of Jesus. See John 2:13-16.) Was that not violent? Was that not aggressive? In addition to this action of Jesus, there are numerous other examples in the Bible where God acts rather violently, such as flooding the earth in the time of Noah and killing all non-aquatic creatures except those aboard the ark (Genesis 6-8); raining down fire upon Sodom and Gomorrah (Genesis 19); killing the firstborn sons of the Egyptians in the time of Moses (Exodus 11-12); and instructing the killing of 3,000 Israelites after the incident with the golden calf (Exodus 32). This is all brutal stuff, but even this pales in comparison to what the Bible claims God will do in the end of days when God will consign the devil and his followers to eternal punishment in the lake of fire (Revelation 20). Anyone who claims the Bible teaches pacifism must first explain why God himself does not follow that moral guide.

The ultimate violent act in the Bible, though, is the cross. Crucifixion, historians tell us, was one of the most painful, brutal, and violent means of execution ever devised by man. According to the Bible, God chose this method to free humans—actually, not just humans but everything within heaven and earth—from the consequences of the fall. The Bible claims that Jesus was "the Lamb that was slain from the creation of the world" (Revelation 13:8). To put this matter succinctly, if God is always against violence, then why the cross?

I once attended a spiritual retreat, held at a monastic center, in an attempt to learn from others how to draw closer to God. I learned many things that were of value, both from participants and from the guest speakers. But while there, I quickly realized the main speaker was an ardent pacifist who found a way, in every lecture, to bring the discussion around to pacifism. In his view, pacifism was always the appropriate action. Even Hitler, he thought, would eventually have been persuaded by pure and devoted pacifism. So I finally asked about the cross: was it not essentially an act of violence on the part of God, or at least an act of violence that God allowed? His response was that the cross was illustrative of the willingness of Jesus to suffer passively, but it was not essential for redemption. I disagreed with him strongly, but I appreciated his consistency. If one opts for philosophical pacifism, one must opt out of orthodox Christianity.

As I understand the Bible, violence is often wrong and even usually is wrong, but there are cases when the best thing to do is to stand up and aggressively fight against evil. To hold the conviction that unilateral pacifism will solve every problem is both naive and non-biblical. If non-Jews had tried to use pacifism to defeat Hitler, the Jewish race would have been annihilated. Six million Jews passively submitted to the Nazis, and it never persuaded Hitler to end his pogrom. Next on Hitler's agenda were the disabled—in fact, a huge eugenics program was already underway in Nazi Germany before the end of the war, ending in the murders of over 200,000 disabled Germans. Any guess who would have come next in the Nazi democides? My guess is the colored races of the world, followed by Muslims, then Christians. In my opinion, it was only the violent response of brave men and women from England, America, and other peace-loving countries that spared millions of innocent people from Hitler's mad course, which would have destroyed our world. Pacifism is simply not a sufficient negotiation tool when dealing with a Hitler, a Stalin, or a group of radical terrorists—especially those who hijack airliners, filled with innocent passengers, and fly them into buildings.

This is not to say that pacifism does not have its place. I greatly respect those who achieved fantastic social changes in their countries by way of pacifism, such as William Wilberforce, Mohandas Gandhi and Martin Luther King, Jr. Maybe this is the lesson learned: when we are dealing with people who respect life and liberty, pacifism can be an effective approach. But when we are dealing with those who have no respect for either life or liberty—when peace is neither possible nor desired—pacifism is an unwise approach.

How can we know peace is not possible?

This is why Paul was inspired to write, in Romans 12:18, "If it is possible, as far as it depends on you, be at peace with all people." How do we know the difference? How do we know when to pursue peace and when to stand up and fight?

I have been greatly helped, over the years, by a saying I was taught in the church in which I was raised,

"In essentials unity; in nonessentials liberty; in all things charity."

This statement is hundreds of years old, and it clearly asserts there are some essentials that are worth fighting for (some say it goes back even to Augustine in the fifth century, though this origin of the phrase is disputed). In our church we apply it this way:

- We believe in the existence of God, on that issue we will not compromise.

- We believe in the divinity and the Lordship of Jesus, that he is the only way to heaven; on that issue we will not compromise.

- We believe in the authority of Scriptures; on that issue we will not compromise.

This is just a partial list, but for us, the essentials are not very numerous. However, there are many other topics, which we label nonessentials (such as end-times theories, church policy issues, etc.), that we are not going to fight over. Occasionally, there are Christians who come to our church who want to argue points of doctrine. I'll be quite honest here: some Christians are just incredibly argumentative. It is just nauseating how much they like to engage in conflict and argue about insignificant things. They may win this or that little doctrinal battle, but they are costing Christians the cultural war. Many churches are divided and many denominations have divided numerous times, causing many non-believers to be turned-off by the apparently ceaseless infighting among Christians. I recently learned that there are ten Presbyterian denominations in the United States, but now, building on what they learned in America, there are now 88 in Korea. As Kathleen Norris noted, "Schism is a dangerous process. Once it starts, there is no end to it."[11]

It seems that we are better at finding reasons to divide than we are at finding reasons to remain unified. All this is in spite of the fact that Jesus prayed that we, his followers, would be unified. He prayed,

> Holy Father, protect them by the power of your name—the name you gave me—so that they may be one as we are one. While I was with them I protected them and kept them safe...
>
> (John 17:11-12)

Jesus clarifies in this passage that unity is something that needs to be protected, and, in fact, he provided that protection for us when he was here on earth, in the flesh. It makes sense, then, that after the resurrection and ascension of Jesus we will need to be protected by something else, hence the armor of God. Jesus clearly prays that God the Father would provide protection for us now; or, to put it conversely, that we should not expect to be able to protect ourselves now. We can rely on God and pray for God's armor, and we can be diligent against those who would destroy the unity of the spirit and the bond of peace.

I remember one man said to me, "What does the church believe about end-times prophecy?"

---

11   Kathleen Norris, *Amazing Grace* (New York: Riverhead Books, 1998), p. 218.

I said, "We don't all have one view of end-times. We have people who have different views in our church."

He replied, "You must be kidding. Aren't you a strong enough pastor to teach the truth?"

So for him, my refusal to argue about non-essentials led him to question my pastoral virility. To say the least, I was not motivated to speak further with him or to understand his views better.

I decided years ago that, as a pastor, I was not going to get drawn into disagreements over things that aren't core issues. Simply put: there is already enough arguing going on in our world. There are already enough denominations. There already have been enough church splits. Don't you agree? So instead of focusing on non-essentials, over which we differ, let's find some stuff to agree upon.

The same is true in marriage: there are some essentials about which a husband and wife have to be unified. One example would be, "In this marriage there will be no affairs." In parenting, there are some essentials as well, such as, "In this household there will be no violence." This is even true on a national level. In America, we are against child abuse, racism, and terrorism, to name just a few. The key is to know which issues are essentials, and which are not.

A great example: Abraham

Abraham was an excellent illustration of this. In Genesis 13, Abraham had a conflict on his hands: Abraham and Lot, Abraham's nephew, went to the promised land with their families, herds and flocks. As their families and flocks increased, they both realized there wasn't enough grass in one area for both of them to thrive. Naturally, their shepherds and herdsman began arguing over the matter: who had the right to use the best pastures? As is so common throughout history, when an issue is financial in nature, serious conflicts arise.

So Abraham was in a pickle, one might say. Abraham knew, since he was both Lot's uncle and older relative, he had the right to pick the best land for himself. If he picked the best land for himself, Lot would probably be upset. He also knew that if he allowed Lot to choose, he might end up with the poorer land, which was much less fertile and filled with hills and more difficult terrain. His shepherds and herdsmen would probably not be happy with that result.

But Abraham was one of those rare individuals who valued family over finances, and who cared more for his friends than he did for power or popularity. He knew the situation was filled with seeds of conflict. So Abraham said to Lot,

> Lot, let there not be conflict between us. You choose which way to go. If you choose the mountains, I will go to the valleys. If you choose the valleys, I will take my family to the mountains. You choose what land you want.
> (Genesis 13:8)

As youth often do, Lot assumed the easy road was the best road, so he chose the fertile, friendly valley. There was one glaring problem with his choice, though. In this valley there happened to be two prosperous cities, named Sodom and Gomorrah. These cities soon became involved in a war in the valley, and all of Lot's possessions were captured. Abraham came to Lot's rescue and won back the lost possessions, but their return was only temporary. These two cities became infamous when God destroyed them due to their moral debauchery, and Lot lost everything of value, including the life of his wife. Abraham, living in the rougher high country, avoided this calamity. Why? It appears that God blessed Abraham for prizing peace more than prosperity, for valuing unity more than property.

Have we made that decision in our own lives? Is peace more important than money? Is unity more important than possessions? Is getting along with others more important than getting our own way?

Forgive me, dear reader, but allow me to be blunt: when people think of you, do they think of someone who always has to win each argument, or do they think of someone who values peace more than winning arguments? When people look at you do they think of someone who values possessions over relationships, or do they think of someone who values unity more than winning?

Let me admit that this has been a hard lesson for me to learn, especially when I was first married. Because of my years studying and teaching philosophy, I often have joked that I have advanced degrees in arguing. But in marriage the ability to argue and debate didn't help a bit. I learned early on that winning arguments with my wife wasn't winning her heart. In fact, the opposite was true: winning arguments tended to push her away. I came to the jarring realization that in many of my former friendships, my competitive nature often led me to win arguments, but it didn't correlate with winning friends.

So with my wife, I developed a little refrain that I would repeat to myself whenever we were discussing a topic, and especially when we were arguing or fighting. The refrain was, "Remember Rick, you love her more than you love winning over her." Or, to put it a different way, I would even say out loud, "Amy, I want your friendship more than I want to win this fight." The results astounded me, and helped make our relationship one that has never been characterized by competition or argument.

I have found the same principles also work with my kids: "Remember, Rick, you value him more than you value victory over him." In contrast, I have seen other parents, who, like me, were raised to be very competitive. Thus, they tend to fight to the bitter end with their kids. They win the arguments with their kids, but they are losing the war for their kids' hearts.

It is so important to value peace more than pride or prosperity. We must make the decision to pray on the shoes of peace. We have to decide, "Hey, I'm going to be a peacemaker. That is who God is, and if God is going to be Lord of my life, this is who God wants me to be."

This approach has helped Amy and me in our marriage. One day, we overslept and were soon irritating each other as we hurried to get the kids ready for school. The irritation escalated into a conflict, then into a heated discussion. Okay, the belt of truth is on, so I'll admit it: we were fighting. Suddenly, in the middle of our fight, Amy had the wisdom to stop and say, "Rick, wait! I've just realized why we are arguing."

My thought was, "Well, I know why we're arguing, but it's probably different than what you are thinking."

She said, "I know why we are arguing, it's the day of the week."

I said, "What do you mean?"

She said, "Today is Tuesday, and early in my prayer time this morning, I prayed for the shoes of peace in my life and in our marriage, just like you taught me to in your sermon."

My first thought was, "I hate when that happens. I hate it when people quote my sermons against me." But quickly, a more Spirit-led thought took control, and I said, "You know, I prayed that very same thing this morning, I prayed for the shoes of peace in my life and in our marriage and family."

In an instant, we both realized that peace was much more important than whatever little conflict over which we were arguing. Our whole argument dissipated, because she prayed for God to arm us with his peace. And it worked! Pray on the shoes of peace, and you will find this carries you through many of the problems and conflicts of life.

Let's try it. First, let's pray about the sorry condition of our world and our overwhelming need for God's peace today. Pray the following prayer aloud, even once or twice if needed to soak deeply into your soul:

Lord,
> This world is full of conflict, quarrels and even wars.
> Though we claim to be people who desire peace,
>> we seem to find no end to the ways we
>> disagree with one another,
>> destroy unity, and demolish community.
> Husbands and wives begin marriages
>> promising undying love to one another,
>> yet too often end in divorce court,
>> dividing up not only bank accounts
>> and household possessions,
>> but also siblings and parents.
> Neighbors fight over trivial matters,
>> politicians fight for power and prestige over principle,
>> and nations fight and sacrifice

the very blood and lives of their young men.
Even Christians find minutiae to argue about,
    dividing into fractured denominations
    and churches split almost like clockwork.
God help us!
We obviously cannot keep the peace on our own,
    and the evil one, the prince of division,
    wins the battles all too often.
We need you, O God, to arm us with your peace.
May the Prince of Peace himself fill our lives,
    may his peace rule in our marriages and families,
    may his peace pervade our communities and nations,
    and may his church emphasize his peace and unity
    more than our non-essential differences.
In the name of Jesus, Amen.

Next, take time to pray individually, by name, for those you love. For instance, I always begin by praying for my wife, then my kids (one at a time), then my parents and siblings, etc. For my wife I pray:

Lord,
    I pray for my wife Amy
        that you would put on her the shoes of peace.
Fill her today, Father, Son and Holy Spirit,
    fill her with the unity of the Trinity,
    fill her with the very love you have shared
    within yourself, O God, from eternity.
When difficult people—especially me!—bring
    conflict into her life,
    help her to be the peacemaker.
When differences and disagreements arise,
    guide her to know what are essentials,
    what are non-essentials,

and how she can always act in love.
In this world where friendships and families seldom last,
    where divorce, betrayals and even wars abound,
    give her the jungle boots of peace,
    strong enough to endure
    the battles the foe will throw at her.
And especially help her know,
    in the deepest parts of her heart and soul,
    that because of Jesus Christ
    she is at peace with you, O God,
    now and forevermore.
And that one day she and her loved ones in Christ,
    will be reunited in Glory and serenity for eternity
In Jesus' name I pray, Amen.

Give this prayer a try, inserting the names of your loved ones. Then sit back, relax, and feel his peace. Thank God that we can trust our loved ones into his care, and that we can rest in his peace. Even though we do not know how specific prayers will be answered and how God will choose to work in particular situations, we are confident in his truth, his righteousness, and his peace.

Pray for your family (or your child's family, or your friend's family):

Lord,
    The evil one seeks to divide and conquer,
        especially husbands from wives,
        and parents from children.
    I pray you would protect the (name) marriage from divorce,
        and the family from fighting and division.
    In Jesus' name, Amen.

Pray for your church (or your child's church, etc.):

Lord,
> The evil one seeks to divide and conquer,
>> including churches and Christian organizations.
> So many churches experience divisions and splits
>> that it must break your heart, O Lord.
> I pray you would protect the (name) church from division,
>> that you would give the leaders unity and wisdom,
>> and the evil one would not gain a foothold there.
> In Jesus' name, Amen.

Pray for your country (or another nation you care about):

Lord,
> The evil one seeks to divide and conquer,
>> including communities, states and even nations.
> I pray you would protect our nation from division,
>> that you would give the leaders unity and wisdom,
>> and the evil one would not gain a foothold here.
> Especially help them know how to protect and defend
>> the freedoms you have endowed upon all humans,
> I pray the leaders will have the wisdom
>> to rarely resort to bloodshed
>> in order to defend those rights and freedoms.
> In Jesus' name, Amen.

This is why I look forward to Tuesdays: after praying, I feel a deep, profound sense of wellness, calm and tranquility. Though there are battles and wars being waged in the spiritual realms around us, I sense that God is in control, and his peace will prevail. It's like my heart and my mind take a deep breath together, sit back together in the easy chair of my soul, and relax. I don't need to solve the problems in the world; instead I pray for myself and those I love to be armed with the shoes of peace. I experience what Paul instructed, "Let the peace that passes all understanding guard your heart and your mind as you trust in Christ Jesus." (Philippians 4:7)

Chapter Five

Wednesday: Wield the Shield of Faith

In previous centuries, to be born on Wednesday was widely believed to be an omen of bad luck. Thomas Nashe, a 16th century playwright and poet, instructed young people in Suffolk, England, that different days of the week were luckier than others,

> "...telling what luck eurie one should have by the day of the weeke he was borne on."

Over time, Wednesday became identified as the unluckiest. This was expressed in a clever limerick, which first appeared in print in 1838 in A. E. Brady's *Traditions of Devonshire*:

> Monday's child is fair of face,
> Tuesday's child is full of grace,
> Wednesday's child is full of woe,
> Thursday's child has far to go,
> Friday's child is loving and giving,
> Saturday's child still works for a living,

But the child who is born on the Sabbath Day
is bonny and blithe and good and gay.

Times and the meanings of words have changed (as the last line especially reveals), but this poem and its lingering influence on popular culture reveals that Wednesday was—and still is—considered to be a bummer of a day.

This notion persists in our modern culture in various forms. John Steinbeck's 1945 novel, *Sweet Thursday* takes its name from the day that comes before it in the novel, "Lousy Wednesday." In the 1970s, the young girl in *The Addams Family* macabre TV comedy was named "Wednesday." In fact, her full name was "Wednesday Friday Addams," since Friday was also considered by some to be an evil day due to the crucifixion. This is also why Paul Revere & the Raiders, a '70s rock & roll band, had a song titled "Wednesday's Child" on their 1970 album *Collage*. The song ended with the words, "Wednesday's child is full of woe. Woe I know, I am Wednesday's child." Even a national TV show to help children in foster homes find permanent adoptive families is called, not surprisingly, *Wednesday's Child*.

Religiously, Wednesday also gets a bad rap. In the Eastern Orthodox Church, Wednesday (in memory of the betrayal of Jesus) is a fast day (along with Friday) in which believers are to abstain from meat. In Western Christianity, Wednesday is best known for the annual "Ash Wednesday," which begins the 40-day fasting period, ending on Palm Sunday. Ashes, in the Bible, represent mourning, which is why Job said to God, "I repent in dust and ashes." (Job 42:6).

And even in secular society, as working people know,

Wednesday is a tough day. As the day begins, the workweek is not yet half over. It is not until noontime that the half-point is reached, sort of the nadir of the weekly journey. This is why the slang term for Wednesday is "hump day."

For Christians who pray on the armor of God daily, however, Wednesday is a wonderful day. The Apostle Paul instructed believers, after they had clothed themselves with truth, righteousness and peace, to "...take up the shield of faith, with which you can extinguish all the flaming arrows of the evil one" (Ephesians 6:16). Since Wednesday begins with a "W," our mnemonic device to remember this particular piece of armor is: *Wednesday: Wield the shield of faith.*

In order to do so, let's begin with our regular, opening prayer:

Lord,
    I am not strong enough to fight the evil one.
    If I try to fight him on my own strength,
        I will fail miserably.
    And if I try to arm myself against him,
        I will fail completely.
    Instead, I ask you to strengthen me, Lord,
        with your mighty power.
    I ask you to put on me the very character of Christ,
        because it's light that overcomes the darkness.
    I ask you to put on me the full armor of God,
        so that I can take my stand against the devil's schemes.
    In Jesus' name, Amen.

One of my favorite pieces of armor

The shield of faith is one of my favorite pieces of the armor of God. I love when Wednesdays come around because faith is such a crucial element in the Christian life—indeed, in every human life—though it is horribly misunderstood by many in our secular society. Faith is one of God's greatest gifts to humans, though it is often maligned by those that call themselves humanists; it is an essential element that enables our rational abilities, though it is often berated by those that call themselves rationalists; it is a key ingredient in discovering what is true, though it is often derided as an enemy of truth.

To be honest, I must quickly admit that faith is sometimes misplaced and mistaken. One such example was the misguided jihad perpetrated by the religious terrorists behind the September 11, 2001 attacks, which certainly gave faith, in the minds of some, a bad name. Historically, some insanely wicked and monstrous things have been done in the name of faith[12], but that is no mortal blow against faith since cold reason also has been used by secularists towards catastrophic ends—just think of the medical and scientific experiments conducted by the Nazis, the gulags of Stalin, or the policies of Mao Tse-Tung.

Yes, in spite of how faith can be misused, it is still an essential ingredient in the Christian struggle through life. Plus, faith brings with it a marvelous benefit: Paul likened faith to a shield "with which you can extinguish all the flaming arrows of the evil one." After learning to pray on the armor of God, many Christians have realized—to their own horror—they've only been partially armed for many years. What a terrible thing to find they have been serving God and yet have been experiencing attack waves of temptations and struggles, because

---

12 Examples of terribly misguided Christian faith include the Crusades, the Inquisition, and witch hunts. If these examples cause you to wonder how God could allow such atrocities, see my book, *31 Reasons to Believe God Exists*, (Roseville, CA: Adventure Publishing, 2011), pp. 107-112.

they were only partially armed. They have been open to attack—unnecessarily. As even Plato once said, "We are twice armed if we fight with faith."

This is why it is so vital, at least one day a week, to pray on the shield of faith. On Wednesdays, I treasure the reminder to pause and pray that God would guide and increase my own faith and the faith of those I love. I pray for the faith of my wife, our children, our friends, our church, our nation, and our world. I pray that all people will truly come to understand and grow in healthy faith. I even pray that atheists, agnostics, philosophers, educators and scientists would all grasp that faith is an essential element in the human rational process, and by recognizing this process they would open themselves to the viability of faith in God.

Let's pray about this:

Lord,
> Misguided people have given faith a bad name,
>> And they have done awful things
>> under the guise of faith.
> As a result, faith is taken to be the opposite of truth;
>> it is seen by many to be an opponent of reason.
> Give me your wisdom, Lord, so I can be a person of
>> both faith and facts,
>> belief and truth,
>> devotion and evidence.
> In Jesus' name, Amen

Faith under fire

It is no news, however, that faith is under fire today. Of course, this is not unique to our times; there have been opponents of faith for centuries. The most vocal and bombastic enemy of faith was the 18th century German philosopher Friedrich Nietzsche. When Nietzsche opined that "Faith means not wanting to know what is true,"[13] he began a *disassociation*, in the minds of non-believers, between faith and truth. After Nietzsche, it became fashionable not only to claim there was a difference between faith and truth, but there was an irreconcilable divorce, an insurmountable chasm between the two.

Benjamin Franklin, who never quite grasped what Biblical faith entailed, also believed there was a stark difference between reason and faith. He said, "The way to see by faith is to shut the eye of reason."[14] To shut one's eyes to the available evidence is, of course, to commit intellectual and scientific suicide. Maybe this is where the notion of "blind faith" arose, but whatever its provenance, 'blind faith' is now considered by many to be a synonym for faith. As the American educator and aphorist (one known for witty aphorisms) Mason Cooley said, "Ultimately, blind faith is the only kind."[15]

Over the last few centuries, a quiet and respectful truce has persisted between those who valued faith and those who thought it was the enemy of reason. The last decade, however, has seen the rise of new and aggressive attacks on faith by some in the atheist camp. The popular science writer Richard Dawkins is one of the most vicious of these new attackers of faith, along with physician Sam Harris, journalist Christopher Hitchens, and a few other rabid anti-theists. In an attempt to debase faith, Dawkins said,

---

13   Nietzsche, *The Portable Nietzsche* (New York: Viking Penguin, 1954), p. 635.
14   Benjamin Franklin, *op. cit.*, p. 245.
15   Mason Cooley, source unknown.

Faith is the great cop-out, the great excuse to evade the need to think and evaluate evidence. Faith is belief in spite of, even perhaps because of, the lack of evidence.[16]

Dawkins also wrote in his book *The Selfish Gene*,

Faith is powerful enough to immunize people against all appeals to pity, to forgiveness, to decent human feelings. It even immunizes them against fear, if they honestly believe that a martyr's death will send them straight to heaven.[17]

Forgive me here for this philosophical aside, but it strikes me odd that Dawkins does not seem to notice that his appeal here to human pity, forgiveness, and other decent values contradicts one of his other famous quotes: "The universe we observe has precisely the properties we should expect if there is, at bottom, no design, no purpose, no evil and no good, nothing but blind pitiless indifference."[18] It is obvious to me that he cannot have it both ways: a pitiless universe and also an appeal to pity, etc. But, I digress. If you, dear reader, are interested in the evidences and reasons for God's existence, I would recommend my book, *31 Reasons to Believe God Exists*.[19]

Joining Dawkins in his tirade against faith is Sam Harris, who has the temerity and self-assurance (faith in his own rational abilities; is this evidence of a contradiction?) to title one of his books, *The End of Faith: Religion, Terror, and the Future of Reason*. In this diatribe, Harris wrote,

---

16   Richard Dawkins, *Untitled Lecture*, Edinburgh Science Festival, 1992.
17   Dawkins, *The Selfish Gene* (Oxford: Oxford University Press, 1989), pp. 330-331.
18   Dawkins, *River Out of Eden* (New York: Basic Books, 1995), p.133.
19   Rick Stedman, *31 Reasons to Believe God Exists*, 2011.

The men who committed the atrocities of September 11 were certainly not "cowards," as they were repeatedly described in the Western media, nor were they lunatics in any ordinary sense. They were men of faith—perfect faith, as it turns out—and this, it must finally be acknowledged, is a terrible thing to be.[20]

Harris also abrogated to himself the authority to decide for us all,

It is time that we admitted that faith is nothing more than the license religious people give one another to keep believing when reasons fail."[21]

Are Harris, Dawkins, Franklin and Nietzsche correct? Is faith opposed to reason? Is it the enemy of evidence and human honesty?

There are many illustrious thinkers, throughout history and even currently, who have thought otherwise. Victor Hugo, author of literary classics such as *Les Miserables* and *The Hunchback of Notre Dame*, said, "Faith is a necessity to man. Woe to him who believes in nothing."[22] Mathematician and philosopher Blaise Pascal said, "Faith indeed tells what the senses do not tell, but not the contrary of that they see. It is above them and not contrary to them."[23] English poet William Wordsworth said in the 19th century, "Faith is passionate intuition,"[24] and Albert Einstein said in the 20th, "Science can be created only by those who are thoroughly imbued with the aspiration toward truth and understanding. This source of feeling, however, springs from the

20   Sam Harris, *The End of Faith* (New York: W. W. Norton & Company, Inc., 2004), p. 67.
21   Harris, *Letter to a Christian Nation* (New York: Alfred A. Knopf, 2006), p. 67.
22   Victor Hugo, *Les Miserables* (New York: Carleton Publisher, 1862), p. 134.
23   Blaise Pascal, *Thoughts* (New York: Collier & Son, 1910), p. 96.
24   William Wordsworth, *The Poetical Words of William Wordsworth* (London: E. Moxar, Son & Co., 1871), p. 458.

sphere of the religious."[25] In other words, science involved an element or attitude of faith for Einstein. My favorite quote about faith, apart from the Bible, is from Dr. Martin Luther King, Jr., who said, "Faith is taking the first step even when you don't see the whole staircase."[26]

Is this not what all of us do in life, every day, both scientists and non-scientists? The decisions to love, to marry, and to have children—are these not steps of faith, in which we proceed without seeing the whole staircase? Is this not what we do when we vote for a certain candidate, or join a club or cause? Is this not what scientists do when they intuit a possible explanation or theory, and then construct experiments to test a hypothesis? They take rational, scientific steps without seeing the whole staircase. Is this not what all science is built upon—basic assumptions about reality that cannot be proven by the scientific method (remember, even the scientific method cannot be proven by the scientific method), such as the orderliness of nature, the repeatability and reliability of cause and effect, etc.?

For instance, it is not possible to prove the axioms of Euclidian geometry—which is why they are called *axioms*. After all, dictionaries define *axioms* as self-evident or universally accepted principles, which means we must adopt them based on faith in human rationality. At the core, science is a faith-based operation, since it is operated by human minds, not computers. At the very least, we must have faith in our own rational ability and in the trustworthiness of science, neither of which can be proven by science.

---

25 Albert Einstein, quoted in Walter Isaacson, Einstein, 2007; quoted in "Einstein and Faith," *Time Magazine*, April 5, 2007.
26 Martin Luther King, Jr., quoted in Zig Ziglar, *The One Year Daily Insights* (Carol Stream, IL: Tyndale House, 2009). p. 319.

A story about Einstein illustrates this point:

A precocious young man once challenged Einstein on this. Einstein, after a short visit, walked outside with the young man and the young man pointed to a tree and said, "Dr. Einstein, how do we know that tree is there?" Einstein's perceptive response was, "Only by faith."[27]

The bottom-line is this: there would be no science, no medicine, no philosophy, no commerce, no communities or cultures, and certainly no marriage or families, if it were not for faith. Faith is a part of every aspect of human life, and it baffles me that Harris, Dawkins and others so blithely throw the baby out with the bathwater.

Why do they do so? It seems to me they begin the observation that terrible things have been done by people of faith. They then conclude that faith itself must be terrible. Remember the above quote of Harris: "They were men of faith¬—perfect faith, as it turns out— and this, it must finally be acknowledged, is a terrible thing to be." This is faulty logic, to say the least. By this rationale, we would be forced to say that since terrible things were done by Nazi doctors, who certainly were educated people of medicine and science, a doctor or scientist is therefore a terrible thing to be. We could claim that terrible things were done by soldiers in the past (which is certainly true), so a soldier is a terrible thing to be (which is certainly false, since it was soldiers who liberated the concentration camp survivors in World War II). The same could be said of business people, bankers, merchants, and even politicians (some people may feel the last case may be the one exception, but again, I digress).

---

27 *Leadership Magazine*, IV, 3, p. 108.

I understand Harris' revulsion at the actions of the 9/11 terrorists, but this clearly seems to me an instance of *bad* faith, not a proof that all faith is bad. Furthermore, there are ample examples of good faith that have produced stellar, revolutionary, morally positive results: Wilberforce, Gandhi, King, Mandela, Mother Teresa, etc.[28]

The key is to make sure one's faith is good faith, not bad; healthy rather than harmful. So here is the key: how are we to be sure that we ourselves are not deceived? How can we be confident we are not self-deluded, and our passionate pursuit is not Mengele-like? How can we be certain we will avoid self-deception?

This is why we don't merely arm ourselves with the shield of faith. Instead, we ask God to put on us his shield of faith. In other words, we ask God himself to shield us, to be our protector, to be a hedge around us.

I'm reminded here of the great scriptural promise found in Psalm 3:3, "But you are a shield around me, O Lord; you bestow glory on me and lift up my head." As the Roman shields, working in concert, formed an impenetrable shield around the soldiers (which we will discuss in a moment), so too the Lord forms such a shield around believers in the spiritual realm. And once again we see that God himself is the shield. To put on the armor of God is not to try and shield ourselves; the armor must come from the hand of God and not the hands of man. We pray for God to put his armor on us, which is to ask that his own person and presence guard us within and without.

If it were merely our own faith, we might be mistaken in some way. No—we always will be mistaken in some way, so we need God's

---

28   This point alone contradicts and therefore disproves the thesis of Christopher Hitchen's book, which is reflected in the title, *God is Not Great: How Religion Poisons Everything*, (New York: Twelve, 2009).

faith to be placed upon and within us, to correct and cleanse away any impure or unhealthy faith. We pray on the armor of God, which always humbles and molds us, rather than we molding it to shape our desires.

If this is the case, doubters may ask, why did it not prevent the 9/11 terrorists? Here is where I need to stress the faith Paul speaks of is not general, religious faith, but specific, Christian faith. Many crazy and criminal things have been done in the name of religious faith. Religions, just like anything else, can be manipulated. So what keeps Christian faith grounded and pure?

It is Jesus himself. We pray on the faith of Jesus, because in this world of confusion, the best we can become is to be like Jesus. Just as we put on the belt of truth, because He is truth; the breastplate of righteousness, because He is our righteousness; and the shoes of peace, because he is the Prince of Peace; we now put on the faith of Jesus. Technically, it would be more proper to speak of not *what* we put on, but *whom*: we put on Christ because Jesus, according to the Bible, is named "Faithful and True" (Revelation 19:11). The author of the book of Hebrews calls Jesus "the author and perfecter of our faith" (Hebrews 12:2). Faith is another aspect of his character, which keeps us from creating our own, mistaken notions of faith, and it keeps us from becoming involved with others who would misguide us about faith.

Here is the glorious and protective outcome: restricting faith to the faith of Jesus keeps and guards us from going astray, from calling some monstrous belief *faith*. In other words, if to have real faith is to grow more and more in the faith of Jesus, we can ask ourselves a simple question: would Jesus have done this? For instance, would Jesus have hijacked a plane and used it as a flying bomb to cause the deaths of thousands of innocent people? Of course not. Anyone doing so is not operating out of proper, Christian faith. In the same way, would Jesus have fought in the crusades, owned slaves, conducted witch trials, or have done other awful things believers have done? Again, of course not. On the other hand, would Jesus pray for miracles of healing, fight against demonic forces, and trust in God when everything in the world seems to go awry? Well, yes. He did those things, so we can infer that those things are proper exercises of faith.

Let's pray about this:

Lord,
>In this world there are many people
>>who claim to have faith.
>But some of them believe outrageous doctrines,
>>and even worse, they behave in atrocious ways.
>In this world, O Lord,
>>how can I be a person of faith and not foolishness?
>The answer, I know, is to be more and more like Jesus.
>Since he is named the "Faithful and True" one,
>>I ask you to fill me with his faith.
>In fact, fill me more and more with the Spirit of Christ
>>so my faith will be his faith,
>>living in and through me.
>In his name I pray, Amen.

The 4th piece of armor: The shield of faith

So we are to ask God to put on us the shield of faith, which we have seen is the faith of Jesus. But what, precisely, is faith?

124

William James, a 19th Century, American philosopher, said "Faith means belief in something concerning which doubt is theoretically possible."[29] At first glance, this appears to be a pretty good definition. If no doubt is possible, there is no need for faith, so faith only exists where there is the potential for doubt. However, even first-year philosophy students quickly learn that there are many things philosophers find to be worthy of doubt. Can we trust our senses to give us an accurate representation of the world? Kant brought that into doubt. Can we trust our sensations of cause and effect, or even our sensations of self? Hume brought those into doubt. Can we trust our experience of reality to be correct? Plato brought that into doubt. Can we trust language to accurately communicate? Quine brought that into doubt. Can we even trust our sensation that we ourselves are real? Berkeley brought that into doubt.

When we start chipping away at the different aspects of human knowledge, we find there are no areas in which doubt is not theoretically possible. Therefore, James' definition of faith proves fruitless in the end. In a way, it is similar to the American Heritage dictionary's definition: faith is "a confident belief in the truth, value, or trustworthiness of a person, idea, or thing." By this definition, Dawkins has faith because he confidently believes in the trustworthiness of science; Harris has faith because he confidently believes in the trustworthiness of his own rational ability; Franklin had faith because he confidently believed in the trustworthiness of the cause of American Revolution. Indeed, by this definition, everyone has some degree of faith.

---

29   William James, *The Will to Believe* (New York: Longmans, Green, & Co., 1919), p. 90.

So the Apostle Paul must have meant something more specific when he instructed the Ephesians to "take up the shield of faith." There must be some sort of biblical faith, which is different from normal epistemic faith. There must be something special about Christian faith to distinguish it from the operational faith essential to human thought and existence.

So what is Christian faith? Theologian and philosopher Thomas Aquinas said, "Just as the idea of faith is to accept what is not seen, so hope means settling for what is not held."[30] Here Aquinas is echoing the Bible, which says, "

> "Now faith is being sure of what we hope for
> and certain of what we do not see."
>
> (Hebrews 11:1)

But even this verse, and the Thomist paraphrase, is more of a description of the results of faith than a definition.

The Bible talks often about faith but does not define it. So we are left to infer its meaning from the lives and examples of those who had it. According to the Apostle Paul, the first great example of a person of faith in the Bible is the patriarch Abraham. In Genesis, God spoke to a man named Abram (later renamed Abraham), then living in the land of Ur (located in what is now southern Iraq). God said, "Leave your country, your people and your father's household and go to the land I will show you. I will make you into a great nation and I will bless you..." (Genesis 12:1-2). Abram obeyed God and went,

---

30 Thomas Aquinas, *Summa Theologiae: Vol. 49, The Grace of Christ* (Cambridge: Cambridge University Press, 2006), p. 17. People often do not recognize that hope is easily understandable in a theistic universe, but not ultimately supported in an atheistic one. See Chapter 13 of my book, *31 Reasons to Believe God Exists*, pp. 101-106.

with his wife, servants and flocks, into the unknown, demonstrating great faith in the process. Later, God came again to Abram and said, "…a son coming from your own body will be your heir. Look up at the heavens and count the stars—if indeed you can count them. So shall your offspring be" (Genesis 15:4-5). This verse is a remarkable testimony of faith because of one important fact: to this point in her life, Abram's wife, Sarai, had been barren.

Then comes the pivotal verse about faith in the Old Testament: "Abram believed the Lord, and he credited it to him as righteousness" (Genesis 15:6). Paul comments on this event with these words:

> What does the Scripture say? "Abraham believed God and it was credited to him as righteousness." … Abraham's faith was credited to him as righteousness.
>
> (Romans 4:3, 9)

So we have here a clear correspondence: In this key sentence, the words "believed God" can be substituted with the word "faith." For Paul, faith is simply living a life based on *believing in God.* It is to live in such a way that belief in God is the guiding, operational theme of one's life. In the words of the prophet Habakkuk, "The righteous will live by faith" (See Habakkuk 2:4 and Romans 1:17). Paul sums this up for the Romans Christians:

> For all have sinned and fall short of the glory of God, and are justified freely by his grace through the redemption that came by Christ Jesus. God presented him as a sacrifice of atonement, through faith in his blood. He did this to demonstrate his justice, because in his forbearance he had left the sins committed beforehand unpunished—he did it to demonstrate his justice at the present time, so as to be

the just and the one who justifies those who have faith in Jesus.

(Romans 3:23-26)

Faith, then, simply means to live out one's belief in God, and even more specifically to believe in God as revealed in Jesus Christ.

This, then, is my definition of Christian faith: it is *to live trusting in the Lord Jesus.* Living in such a way is a declaration that God, as revealed in Jesus, is more dependable than we are, that his will is better for us than our own, and that his ways are more just (Isaiah 55:6-56:1). We choose to trust in God rather than in ourselves. As Oswald Chambers said, "faith is deliberate confidence in the character of God, whose ways you may not understand at the time."[31]

What does it mean to live trusting in God?

What does this entail, to live trusting in God more than ourselves? As we have already noted in previous chapters, the Bible is clear that we cannot trust ourselves. The prophet Jeremiah said, "The heart is deceitful above all things and beyond cure. Who can understand it?" (Jeremiah 17:9). Solomon, known as the wisest person who ever lived, was wise enough to not trust in his own wisdom. He said,

> Trust in the Lord with all your heart,
>   and do not lean on your own understanding;
> In all your ways acknowledge him,
>   and he will make your paths straight.
> Do not be wise in your own eyes;

---

31 Oswald Chambers, quoted in Sean McDowell, *Apologetics Study Bible for Students* (Nashville: Holman Christian Standard Bible, 2009), p. 843.

fear the Lord and shun evil.
This will bring health to your body
    and nourishment to your soul.

(Proverbs 3:5-8)

Solomon also said,

Do you see a man wise in his own eyes?
    There is more hope for a fool than for him.

(Proverbs 26:12)

In a similar vein, the prophet Isaiah said,

Woe to those who are wise in their own eyes,
    and clever in their own sight...
Therefore, as tongues of fire lick up straw
    and as dry grass sinks down in the flames,
so their roots will decay
    and their flowers blow away like dust;
for they have rejected the law of the Lord Almighty
    and spurned the word of the Holy One of Israel.

(Isaiah 5:21, 24)

I love that phrase: "Do not be wise in your own eyes." Is there any truth more misunderstood in today's secular society than this? In this postmodern era, is there any maxim we are more blind to than this? The true evidence of wisdom, according to the Bible, is that we can't trust our own wisdom. Instead, we realize that God—not ourselves—is the source and fount of all wisdom, and we seek to know his will and his ways. As Solomon also wrote,

The fear of the Lord is the beginning of wisdom,
    and knowledge of the Holy One is understanding.

(Proverbs 9:10)

129

Deep down inside our souls, I believe we all know this to be true: we have, at crucial moments in our lives, led ourselves terribly astray. We all have made decisions that, in hindsight, clearly were very poor ones. We all have done deeds that we regret, actions that have brought deep pain into the hearts and lives of others. One of the most difficult, yet necessary, realizations in life is: "I really can't trust myself to always know what is best, or to even do what is best when I know it. I need a guide in life, a shepherd who sees the bigger picture and can give me direction and guidance."

Because of this, King David famously prayed,

> The Lord is my shepherd,
>   I shall not be in want.
> He makes me lie down in green pastures,
>   he leads me beside still waters,
>   he restores my soul.
> He guides me in paths of righteousness
>   for his name's sake...
>
> (Psalm 23:1-3)

Here is the crux of the matter, and what I think really bothers atheists such as Dawkins and Harris about faith: to have faith in God means to believe in God more than we believe in ourselves. For those that have trusted in themselves and in their own rational abilities, this comes as a Copernican change, a major paradigm shift regarding our mental abilities. As philosopher Alvin Plantinga has shown, to trust in one's own rational ability is not supportable within a Darwinian framework anyway.[32] Even within the evolutionary worldview, evolutionists must be very cautious about trusting ultimately in the

---

32   Alvin Plantinga, Belief in God and Proper Warrant, (Oxford: Oxford University Press, 1993).

cognitive abilities of evolving creatures. This is why leading thinkers, such as C. S. Lewis, have spoken of evolution as self-defeating: if it is right, then it is incapable of asserting that it is right.[33]

This is another of those interesting philosophical asides that beckons our attention; but instead of running down that trail, let me return to my central point: faith is to trust in God rather than in oneself. This brings us to the Rubicon that Dawkins and his ilk just can't seem to cross: to choose to believe in God more than we believe in our own rational ability. This means we will believe in God's will more than in our will. It means we will believe in God's Word more than in our own words (we will discuss further in Chapter Seven, which deals with "Fight with the sword of the Spirit, which is the Word of God"). Ultimately we hold the belief that we need to rely on God to save us rather than depend on our own ability. True faith is to receive and follow the Savior he has offered—his Son, Jesus Christ.

Why is faith likened to a shield?

I have often wondered why faith is likened to a shield, which Paul says protects us not just from the attacks of evil, but from "all" the flaming darts of the evil one. How is this possible? A shield can certainly protect us from arrows launched towards us, if our shield is in front of us. But if it is in front, how can attacks from the side or rear be prevented, for surely Satan attacks believers from all angles? In fact, I would guess the evil one especially likes to surprise and attack from the rear, stabbing people in the back, so to speak.

---

33 For more on this see C. S. Lewis, *Mere Christianity* (New York: Macmillan Pub., 1943); Victor Reppert, *C. S. Lewis' Dangerous Idea* (Downer's Grove, IL: Intervarsity Press, 2003); Tim Keller, *The Reason for God* (New York: Dutton, 2008); and Plantinga, op. cit.

The answer to this question is found in understanding the purpose of a shield in Roman armament and warfare, and the type of shield Paul specified in Ephesians 6:16. There were two different kinds of shields the Romans used: a small shield used in hand to hand combat (called *aspis* in Greek or *clipeus* in Latin) and a large shield which could not be carried in hand to hand combat. Instead, the large shield was only used when the soldiers were fighting together, as a unit, in formation.

It is this second type of shield, the *thureos*, which Paul specified in Ephesians 6:16. A *thureos* was made of wood and covered with leather, which, before taken into battle, would be soaked in water. In this way the leather would be stronger and less brittle. Plus, the wet leather had an added benefit: the water helped to douse and extinguish any flaming arrows.

A *thureos* was a big shield. This Legionary shield was tall and oblong, approximately 2-½ feet wide by 4 feet tall.[34] In fact, the root of the Greek word *thureos* was *thura*, which literally meant "door" or "gate" in Koine Greek. In other words, the shield was like carrying around the door of one's house!

Why were these shields so large? The answer is inspiring: as the Roman soldiers marched together in formation, they kept one another safe from enemy arrows by walking shield-to-shield-to-shield. In this fashion, a legion of Roman soldiers could march up to a city wall or an enemy's front line and be impervious to the arrows shot at them by opposing archers. Even if the soldiers were surrounded during battle, they could completely enclose themselves within their shields

---

34   Fields, *op. cit.*, p. 191.

by constructing an instant defensive barrier like a turtle's shell, under which the soldiers could hide. In antiquity, such a military formation was called a phalanx, which the 300 Spartans used with great, albeit temporary, success in renowned battle of Thermopylae.

Here's the point: the shield of faith was never meant to be used by solo Christians. The shield of faith is to be used in formation, alongside other Christians who have also taken up their shield, their *thureos* of faith. To do so takes coordination, cooperation and, supremely, a real sense of trust. Soldiers had to be certain their fellow legionnaires would not falter or fade back due to fear; their mutual lives literally depended upon how well each one held up his *thureos*.

Obviously, we 21st century Christians could learn from their example. Many Christians today think they can be Lone Ranger Christians. They sincerely believe they don't need to belong to a church; they can just visit around, hop and shop, pop in or out, and participate when and where they desire. They genuinely think they don't need others or to become members. They can study the Bible on their own; they can pray on their own; they can even worship on their own.

The problem is they leave themselves massively undefended. We can be sure their enemy, the evil one, knows exactly when and where they are susceptible, and we can also be sure he won't fight by the rules of gentleman combat. Solo Christians eventually will be attacked by the evil forces, and will find flaming arrows coming in at them from all sides. They will be deeply wounded. They are vulnerable.

Plus, solitary believers render themselves a non-threat to the enemy. They cannot advance upon a city wall alone, they cannot frighten and defeat the enemy, they cannot wreak the havoc a unified force can (see Joel 2:1-2, 7-11). In other words, both spiritual warfare and evangelism suffer when Christians are not strongly tied to one another in authentic Christian community.

The key is this: we Christians—each one of us—need to be vital and viable parts of a local church, a local body of Christ, and not just the church universal. Visitors occasionally tell me, "I don't need to be a member of a particular church; I'm a member of the world-wide body of Christ." That may be sufficient for salvation, but it is a poor strategy to fight the evil one on this side of Glory.

In a culture that devalues church commitment and membership, I relentlessly and tirelessly call people to commit to church membership *each and every week* in our church services. Yes, you read that correctly. We worship, we pray, we celebrate communion, we saturate ourselves with the Word, we call on people to be saved— and we call on Christians to commit to church membership. I believe deeply that Christians need to be committed to membership in their local churches, quite parallel to how spouses are called to committed faithfulness in their marriages. When we decide to love someone, it's for the long haul. And when we decide to be part of a family, a community, it too should be an enduring commitment.

This is what church membership means to me: not merely having one's name on a roll or register somewhere, but being intimately and closely connected to other believers in long-lasting and faithful relationships. Membership means committing to and participating in a local church, being a part of a small group within the church—

an accountability group—close enough to confess and pray with one another. Membership means not moving from church to church when one youth group is better than another, or even when one preacher is better than yours.

By the way, what do parents who change churches every few years teach their kids? Right…that long-term commitment is not needed in churches. This is what the church provided in days gone by; church friends were for life. Church members became honorary family members, and though they were often irritating, they were never abandoned. As they knew better than to abandon a blood-family, they also knew not to abandon a church family.

Sadly, people today do both. This, of course, has ripple effects. Today's children may grow up without the ability to stick with a specific group of people, other than their biological family, for an extended period of time (and maybe not even their own family unit). Children raised in families without long-term church commitment may be liable to become opportunists that treat churches like shopping at Kmart or Walmart; church becomes just a matter of convenience and economics rather than discipleship, loyalty, or long-term community building.

On the other hand, children who have been taught to stick with their local church through thick and thin—everything except heresy— will be better equipped to make it through the difficult seasons that will surly arise in their own future lives and families. Long-term church families provide a network of friendships, which in turn provide models and examples for younger kids. Furthermore, they supply a strong Christian and time-proven peer group during the crucial teen years.

Plus, when tempted in sundry ways, active church membership holds people *accountable*. Long-term friends hear that a couple is struggling in their marriage, and they come alongside them, praying for them, encouraging them not to quit. Long-term fellow-members hear of an illness and they are there in the hospital, praying with the family. Long-term church members hear of a death in a church family, and they are ready with meals and offers to help in any way. Church members hear of a fellow member in distress, and they are there to help and serve.

I clearly remember one church family whose home was flooded after torrential rains in our area; the waterline in the house was, as I remember it, about four feet high. Everything they owned was filled with water, mud, and debris, and from it all emanated an awful odor. To make matters worse, everything had to be washed and sterilized due to the possibility of bacteria in the water. Our church heard of their plight, and, as soon as the water receded, our members were at their home. Couples descended on the home, taking garbage bags of clothes home to launder. Carpenters put furniture items in their trucks to repair and repaint. Adults and children cleaned walls and floors. The house was like a beehive, with church members buzzing all around. There were tears and sadness to be sure, but there were also smiles and laughter, and the sense that all would be well. We would conquer this problem—together. All would be well.

As I took one load of laundry outside, I noticed the stark contrast on the neighbor's lot: there stood a husband and wife alone, trying to clean up but barely making a dent in the mess. No friends were there helping, no trucks hauling, no volunteers cleaning. I wondered: had this family often thought, "We don't need to go to church. Churches are only out to take people's money. We can worship God here by ourselves, or at least watch a church service on TV." When the winds and floods literally came, their support was nowhere to be seen. In that moment, I became more convinced than ever that the church was not only the vehicle created by God through which the world was to be saved, but the local church was the solution by which life becomes survivable.

But pertinent to the topic of this chapter, membership means that when the enemy attacks, someone has our back! We are not caught off guard by the flaming darts of the evil one, for we have a praying and caring community around us. The local body of Christ, as together we have prayed on the *thureos* of faith, becomes a supernatural supershield, protecting one another together more completely than any of us could do alone.

So pray the armor of God on those you love! You know they will be tempted and attacked—every day—by the evil one in this dark and twisted world. So pray that God would put on them his shield of faith, and help them understand our spiritual shields are only effective when Christians operate in teams. In other words, pray they realize that believers are most vulnerable when alone. Pray that they grow to profoundly grasp that Christianity is a group enterprise. We are not to be Lone Rangers; we are not to be Han Solos. If we are to be adequately protected in this world of evil, we must be committed, active, and regular church members. Please pray the following prayer with me aloud:

Lord,
    My loved ones need protection in this world of evil,
        the fiery darts of the evil one
        are loaded and aimed towards them.
    They need you to be a shield around them.
    So I pray you put on them, today and every day,
        your shield of faith,
        which you have promised will protect them from
        all the flaming arrows of the enemy.
    Help them also to fully understand
        that their shield was never designed to be used alone.
    It only works when they are in group formation,
        working together as a spiritual team, a family.
    In other words, they need to be church members:
        committed, involved, enduring church members.
    Lead them to a Christ-centered, Bible-based, Spirit-filled
        church in which they can be treasured and challenged,
        a church in which they will be accountable.
    Protect them, O God,
        in your will and for your glory.
    In Jesus' name, Amen.

I love praying this for those I love. On Wednesdays, I pray for my wife, our marriage, and our kids—child by child. I pray for our relatives, our church and our nation. I pray that God puts his shield of faith around us all. I pray that God would help us grow to understand the value of faith. I pray that those I love will come to deeply believe one of the smartest things they can do is to have faith in God, and to live every moment of their lives in light of that faith. I pray that God himself would be a shield about them, to protect them from all the fiery darts of the evil one. I pray God would help them to grow in the assurance of faith and grow to doubt, less and less, what the Bible says. I pray he would help them to learn that living according to his Word is one of the smartest ways to live. I pray that those I love will be people who walk in step with other believers and thus become strong, because they are not alone on the battlefield. Finally, I pray the church of Jesus Christ might become stronger than ever before, filled with committed members who will love, serve and protect each other as a team, through the ups and downs of life, until the Lord himself calls us home to Glory. What a great way to pray!

Chapter Six

Thursday: Think Within the Helmet of Salvation

The Brain - is wider than the Sky -
For - put them side by side -
The one the other will contain
With ease - and You - beside....
The Brain is just the weight of God -
For - Heft them - Pound for Pound -
And they will differ - if they do -
As Syllable from Sound.
~Emily Dickinson

"An idle brain is the devil's workshop." This well-known proverb is not from the Bible, but is an English adage that can be traced back to the early 1600s. In a compilation of sermons and articles known as *The Works of William Perkins*,[35] the English Puritan minister was the first to record this phrase (in the quaint and pre-standardized spelling of his day): "The idle bodie and the idle braine is the shoppe

---

35   I love the full title of Perkins' *Works*, published in 1603, which I find refreshing in our age of sound bites and catchy titles: "*The works of that famous and worthie minister of Christ, in the Universitie of Cambridge, M.W. Perkins : gathered into one volume, and newly corrected according to his owne copies. With distinct chapters, and contents of euery book, and a generall table of the whole.*"

of the deuill."[36]

A few centuries later, Thomas Fuller, a physician who is best known for his books of collections of proverbs, recorded in *Gnomologia*, "Idle Brains are the devil's Workhouses."[37] The common form of the saying, "An idle brain is the devil's workshop," is first found in the *Hand-Book of Proverbs*, a collection published in 1855 by H. G. Bohn.[38]

From this point, the phrase "The devil's Workshop" entered popular culture, and now has been used as the title for novels, movies, comic books (a dangerous neighborhood in Batman's Gotham City is called this), a non-fiction memoir of a Nazi counterfeiting operation, a sound studio in Minnesota, a jewelry store in Canada, an online knife-makers club, and a tobacco shop in California. In other words, in modern parlance "The devil's Workshop" is no longer a bad thing.

But could this be *true*? If there is such a being as the devil (Christians believe this is the case, as Jesus also certainly did), is the mind a place in which the devil not only can freely roam, but make his own workplace or studio? Is the brain the location in which the real wrestling match, the tug of war between good and evil, takes place?

Yes, according to the Bible. There is a battle going on in the minds of human beings.

Let's pause a moment and pray about this:

---

36 William Perkins, *Works* (1603), p. 906. Perkins also was the author of the Latin phrase, *fidei vita vera vita*, which means, "The true life is the life of faith." If a person were to memorize only one Latin phrase, this would be a good candidate.
37 Thomas Fuller, *Gnomologia* (1732), no. 3053. *Gnomologia* is made up of two root words, *gnomos* meaning a short or brief saying, and *logia* meaning a study of a certain topic.
38 H.G.Bohn, *Hand-Book of Proverbs* (1855), no. 311.

Lord,
>
>>People today don't take your existence seriously
>>>and they even are flippant and casual
>>>when talking about your enemy, the devil.
>>They act as if life is a big game, as if existence is like
>>>an appearance on *The Price is Right*
>>>or a spin on *The Wheel of Fortune* TV show.
>>But life is not a game,
>>>and the consequences are eternal.
>>So I ask you to put your full armor, O God,
>>>on me and on those I love.
>>We need your protection from the enemy,
>>>especially our minds, thoughts and attitudes.
>>Put on us your helmet of salvation, O Lord,
>>>so we can think clearly and correctly.
>>In Jesus' name, Amen.

The Apostle Paul said in his second letter to the Christians in Corinth,

>The god of this age has blinded the minds of unbelievers,
>so that they cannot see the light of the gospel that displays
>the glory of Christ, who is the image of God.
>
>>(2 Corinthians 4:4)

In this verse, the Bible clearly teaches the very thing we are considering: the god of this age (the devil) not only is able to penetrate the minds of human beings, but he already has "blinded," in fact, the minds of those who do not believe. This is why, dear Christian reader, what seems so crystal clear to you will, at the same time, appear completely ludicrous to your non-believing friends or family. It will be perfectly clear to you that God exists; others will find this a concept too difficult to accept. You will instantly recognize the voice of God speaking through Scripture; others will find the Bible difficult to understand or nonsense all together. You will be touched in a worship service and feel the very presence of God; others will sense absolutely nothing at all. You will feel the call of God to sacrifice your life for his cause; others will see this as insanity and suicidal. The reason for today's intellectual disjunction is that human beings are very capable of being deceived.

Lest we Christians become smug, let me quickly point out that we are not immune to the devil's deceptions. The Bible claims that this can happen to Christians too. In that same letter to the Corinthians, Paul wrote:

> But I am afraid that just as Eve was deceived by the serpent's cunning, your minds may somehow be led astray from your sincere and pure devotion to Christ.
>
> (2 Corinthians 11:3)

Yes, our minds can be led astray. We must be diligent to recognize our own propensity to be deceived and even self-deceived. The Bible claims the devil is constantly on the prowl, so to speak, looking for those he can lead astray, which is the first step towards his ultimate intention to destroy and "devour." How can we prevent him from doing this? Peter instructs:

> Be alert and of sober mind. Your enemy the devil prowls around like a roaring lion looking for someone to devour.
>
> (1 Peter 5:8)

Our enemy is so subtle, so conniving and so shrewd, that we must keep ourselves in a constant state of mental clarity. There is a battle going on for our thoughts; there is a war being waged for control of our minds.

How is this battle being waged? In today's culture, we are bombarded mentally by the messages conveyed to us through the various forms of media (such as TV, radio, magazines, the Internet, billboards, etc.), which are themselves laced through and through with marketing and advertising campaigns. Studies show the average person is exposed to over 3,000 advertisements a day[39], and the number seems to be exponentially increasing on a yearly basis.

Television, of course, is a primary battle zone in the war for thoughts and minds. Television programs are interrupted every few minutes to run ads to convince us to buy this or that product, support this candidate or that cause, or tune in to yet another program. These ads run at a cumulative cost of approximately $250 billion per year, trying to market over 900,000 brands.[40]

If we desire to win the battle for the minds of those we love, we must somehow find a way to protect those minds. How can we protect our brains and thoughts against the perpetual bombardment this world has to offer?

In the physical world, the solution is helmets, which are becoming more and more common in popular culture today. When I was a kid, the only helmets I remember wearing were batting and football helmets; no one wore a helmet when riding bikes, and very few adults wore them on their motorcycles. Today, there are laws

---

39 The American Academy of Pediatricians reported "young people view more than 40,000 advertisements per year on television alone," and over 3,000 per day when all advertisements in our culture are considered. http://aappublications.org/content/118/6/2563.full (accessed 02/02/2012).
40 *Ibid.*

(in California) that require motorcyclists to wear helmets, so even libertarian 'easy riders' no longer have the freedom to feel the breeze through their hair as they ride their Harleys. Children are legally forced to wear helmets when bicycling and when skateboarding at public skateparks. Though I am unaware of states that currently requiring helmets for snowboarding or skiing (Sonny Bono may have survived his skiing accident had he been wearing a helmet), this is rather easy for parents to demand of our children since we parents usually pay the cost of their lift tickets. I've even seen helmets on kids playing in soccer leagues! Helmets are quite common today since parental protectiveness seems to have kicked into high gear. Kids soon may think of them as an ordinary piece of everyday attire.

One of my favorite stories illustrates this point. A family was out for a Saturday drive and happened to see, along the highway, a sign advertising "Nature Park: 3 miles off next exit." The father was an outdoorsman, and immediately decided a walk in a park was just what they needed. With his wife beside him and his young kids in the backseat, he turned off the highway and began following signs down a country road. He saw a few bicyclists coming towards them, and as they passed by he suddenly realized what "Nature Park" meant: they weren't wearing *any* clothes. Shocked into silence, the father nonetheless had the presence of mind to stop the car, navigate a tight U-turn, and head back towards the highway—which meant they had to pass the cyclists again. The family passed again in silence, the father wondering at the impact this would have on his kids. Finally one boy spoke up in disbelief: "Dad, did you see those people? They weren't wearing any helmets."

How to protect the minds of those we love

Fortunately, God designed a piece of his armor to protect our spiritual minds: the helmet of salvation. The helmet was, in the panoply of Roman armament, the piece designed to protect one's fragile and vital head. One can lose a limb or be painfully injured in many parts of the body and yet survive. But obviously, the same cannot be said about one's head. If one's head is vulnerable, survival itself is at risk.

Because of this, Roman military helmets were an essential part of the panoply. They usually were fashioned out of bronze, which was a malleable metal and relatively easy to mold to fit one's head. Wealthier soldiers had helmets forged out of iron, which involved a more difficult forging process but produced a more durable and hard to penetrate material. Poorer soldiers often wore helmets made of inexpensive leather, or several layers of leather for extra strength. A soldier could even fashion a leather helmet for himself and thus avoid the expense of a blacksmith. Ultimately, there was no excuse to go into battle with one's head unprotected.

Early Roman helmets consisted of what I would term a simple 'shell' or 'bowl' that covered one's cranium, which we might compare today to the shape of a modern baseball cap, minus the bill (also called the brim). To protect one's neck, there was attached to the back of the basic helmet a "shelf," similar to a baseball bill but affixed to the rear of the shell. The purpose of this rear shelf was to protect the soldier's neck and shoulders from above and from the rear. Think of a baseball cap worn backwards: the brim then provided a similar shelf to shield one's neck from the sun, and more importantly from arrows descending from behind or above. This shelf was made out of metal or leather, and was securely fastened to the back of the helmet.

The Roman helmet also had "cheek-pieces" to protect the sides of one's face, but these were not inflexibly attached to the helmet, as they were in Greek helmets. The Greeks had decreased visibility and mobility due to the rigidity of their helmets, but the Romans solved this problem. The Romans fastened metal or leather plates with hinges, above each cheekbone, to provide protection and also better movement than stationary cheek-pieces. These coverings protected the sides of one's face and were connected at the bottom with a leather strap—sort of a chinstrap, if you will. This strap held the cheek-pieces in place, and also provided the extra benefit of cinching down the whole helmet so it remained securely on the soldier's head during battle.

During the first century, Roman soldiers sometimes added a small "bill" to the front of the helmet, probably to protect their eyes from the intense middle-eastern sun that made visibility difficult not only during battles, but also during their long marches. They also added ear coverings made of bronze, if such could be afforded.

The purpose of a spiritual helmet

If the purpose of the Roman helmet was to protect a soldier's head and most importantly his brain—without which one obviously would not survive—then what is the purpose of the helmet in the spiritual armor of God? In a sense parallel to the value of a helmet for a soldier, we could summarize the importance of a spiritual helmet as two-fold:

    1. a spiritual helmet protects one's mind and thoughts,

2. a spiritual helmet therefore protects the survival of one's soul.

Let's discuss the second reason for a helmet's value first. The head required protection because without one's head, survival is impossible. In the Bible, this is illustrated by the idiomatic phrase, "cut off the head," which meant not just to take someone's life, but to thoroughly conquer and kill an opponent. The young David, as he stood before the giant warrior Goliath, boasted,

> This day the LORD will deliver you into my hands, and I'll strike you down and *cut off your head*. This very day I will give the carcasses of the Philistine army to the birds and the wild animals, and the whole world will know that there is a God in Israel.
>
> (1 Samuel 17:46)

In other words, David was not merely going to defeat Goliath; he would embarrass and dispose of him so that neither Goliath's reputation nor his remains would survive. In the same way, after he defeated Goliath and later succeeded Saul as king, King David was confronted by a man named Shimei, a commoner from the clan of Saul. Brazenly, Shimei began to curse the King and even "pelted David and all the king's officials with stones." This was a defiant effort to humiliate the King. The Bible records,

> Then Abishai son of Zeruiah said to the king, "Why should this dead dog curse my lord the king? Let me go over and *cut off his head*."
>
> (2 Samuel 16:9)

Abashai did not want to merely have a talk with Shimei and

convince him to be silent; he did not even want to force him to stop throwing rocks. Abashai wanted to kill him in such a way that would rescue the King David's honor.

A final example of this is when the prophet Elisha was threatened by Ben-Hadad, the King of Aram. "[The King] said, 'May God deal with me, be it ever so severely, if the head of Elisha son of Shaphat remains on his shoulders today!' " The text goes on to say,

> Now Elisha was sitting in his house, and the elders were sitting with him. The king sent a messenger ahead, but before he arrived, Elisha said to the elders, "Don't you see how this murderer is sending someone to *cut off my head?* Look, when the messenger comes, shut the door and hold it shut against him. Is not the sound of his master's footsteps behind him?"
>
> (2 Kings 6:32)

The point of these three examples is this: without one's head, one cannot survive. This is why, I believe, Paul called the spiritual helmet in the armor of God the "helmet of salvation." Without salvation, one will not survive spiritually—especially beyond the grave.

Of course, salvation is one of, if not the most, important topics in the Bible. According to the Bible, all human beings have fallen from our Edenic design, and now are sinners. As Paul put it famously to the Christians in Rome, "There is no one righteous, not even one," and "All have sinned and fall short of the glory of God" (Romans 3:10, 23). Such sinful people deserve spiritual and eternal death, according to the Bible: "Although they know God's righteous decree that those who do such things deserve death, they not only continue to do these very things but also approve of those who practice them." (Romans 1:32)

What will happen when we die?

What a surprise this will be to modern people when they die! Now, I don't mean by this that contemporary people will be surprised, after passing away, that there is life after death. Though we live in an increasingly secular age, polls still clearly show that almost everyone still believes in the existence of God and of the afterlife. Fox News reported in 2004 that Americans overwhelmingly believe in the existence of God (92%), in the reality of heaven (85%) and in the possibility of miracles (82%). These percentages have remained relatively stable over the past several decades, but an unexpected reversal has occurred in the percentage of those that believe in the existence of the devil and hell. In a stunning recovery, belief in the reality of the devil rose from 63% in 1997 to 71% in 2004. Equally surprising was the cause of this new trend: it was due to a rise among *young* people—86% of young adults (ages 18 to 34) claimed to believe in hell, as opposed to 68% of those over the age of 70. Fox News noted, "Similarly, 79% of young people believe in the devil compared to 67% of the over-70 age group."[41]

But many of these believers in the supernatural assume they will automatically go to heaven when they die. In 2005, ABC News reported poll results which revealed 89% of all surveyed believe in the existence of heaven (up a few points from the previous year's Fox poll), and a full 85% think they will go there. The poll also revealed that even the vast majority of non-religious people believe they will go to heaven

---

41   http://www.foxnews.com/story/0,2933,99945,00.html#ixzz1k747jFyQ (accessed 01/21/2012).

after death: 72% of non-religious people believe heaven is real, and 77% believe they will end up there.[42]

When asked about the reasons people will end up in heaven, a recent Barna Group poll reported: "Most Americans believe they, themselves, will go to heaven. Yet, when asked to describe their views about the religious destiny of *others*, people become much less forgiving." Specifically, the poll found that 40% felt all humans would go to heaven because God loves everyone, and 48% agreed that "If a person is generally good or does enough good things for others, they (*sic*) will earn a place in heaven."[43]

These beliefs are startling, to say the least. The first is easily dismantled by asking, "Does this mean you believe people like Hitler and Stalin will be in heaven?" If this is so, it is difficult to retain any notion of prevailing justice, and even the concept of the Lord as a just God.

Because of this, the more common belief is that "good people" will go to heaven. Over the years, I have had many discussions with non-believers about heaven, and almost every person has said some form of "I'll go to heaven because I've been a pretty good person in this life." (As an aside, notice that in order to judge oneself as 'pretty good,' one must have some scale of justice upon which to measure goodness, which entails the existence of an objective gradient of justice. This is impossible if God is not a God of justice, which further supports our discussion in the previous paragraph.)

Here is the important point about heaven and pretty good

---

42 http://abcnews.go.com/US/Beliefs/story?id=1422658 (accessed 01/21/2012).
43 http://www.barna.org/faith-spirituality/484-what-americans-believe-about-universalism-and-pluralism (accessed 01/21/2012).

people: the Bible clearly teaches that heaven is a perfect place and no imperfect person will be allowed in. For instance, the Apostle John prophesied in Revelation,

> I saw a new heaven and a new earth, for the first heaven and the first earth had passed away... I saw the Holy City, the new Jerusalem, coming down out of heaven from God, prepared as a bride beautifully dressed for her husband. And I heard a loud voice from the throne saying, "Now the dwelling place of God is with men, and he will live with them. They will be his people, and God himself will be with them and be their God. He will wipe every tear from their eyes. There will be no more death or mourning or crying or pain, for the old order of things has passed away. He who was seated on the throne said, "I am making everything new!" Then he said, "Write this down, for these words are trustworthy and true."
>
> (Revelation 21:1-5)

In the rest of the chapter, John was given a tour of the celestial city, guided by an angel (21:9). He saw the famous gates of pearl and streets of gold (21:21), and also the river of the water of life and the tree of life (22:1-2). He noticed there was no temple in heaven, for "the Lord Almighty and the Lamb are the temple" (21:22). He also noted "The city does not need the sun or the moon to shine on it, for the glory of God gives it light, and the Lamb is its lamp," (21:23) and "there will be no night there" (21:25).

John then summarized,

Nothing impure will ever enter it, nor will anyone who does what is shameful or deceitful, but only those whose names are written in the Lamb's book of life.

(Revelation 21:27)

This is the crux of the matter: nothing and no one impure will be allowed into heaven. Dear friend, that leaves you and me out. That leaves every person out who has ever lived except one—Jesus himself, the only perfectly pure person. The rest of us fall into the impure category, which excludes us from heaven.

Why is this? Is God not a loving God? Doesn't he want us in heaven? The answer to both questions is yes, so the issue is not the character of God. Instead, the answer is the composition of heaven. Think about this rationally: if heaven is a perfect place, what would happen if one pretty good, albeit imperfect, person were allowed entrance? heaven would no longer be a perfect place. One impure person would spoil the perfection of the new Eden, just as the sins of Adam and Eve spoiled the first. And consider what would happen when another pretty good person was admitted... and another... and another... and another. Sooner or later these imperfect people would conflict about something, over time the number of conflicts and their intensity would escalate, and we would eventually end up with the same hell that we now have on earth. One little sin in the original Eden launched the landslide that has resulted in the crime and chaos we have today. There is no rational reason to suppose the same would not happen again.

So will 'pretty good' people get into heaven? I often attempt to point out to those who are banking on this that their hope is not

153

even logical. I'm reminded here of the mother who was shocked to learn her kids were interested in trying marijuana. She said, "It's bad for you," to which they responded, "A little bit won't matter." So she devised an ingenious plan.

She prepared a fresh pan of brownies, and took them out of the oven just before the kids arrived home. The delectable smell filled the air, and the kids rushed to the kitchen. Just before they took their first bite, the mother said, "Wait. I prepared these brownies a little differently than usual. I put just a little bit of dog poop in the mix. But don't worry, a little bit won't matter."

The kids, of course, refused to eat the brownies. They proved by their own actions that a little bit of impurity does make a big difference, and the same will be true in heaven. Dear friend, the only way to get into heaven, for people like you and me who have lived imperfect lives, is to be purified. This is not something we can do for ourselves. The Bible teaches that this is not only what Jesus can do, but it also is exactly why he came to earth in the first place. This is a theme in the book of Hebrews:

> The Son is the radiance of God's glory and the exact representation of his being, sustaining all things by his powerful word. After he had provided *purification* for sins, he sat down at the right hand of the majesty in heaven.
>
> (Hebrews 1:3)

> In bringing many sons to glory, it was fitting that God, for whom and through whom everything exists, should make the author of their salvation *perfect* through suffering... Although he was a son, he learned obedience from what he

154

suffered and, once made perfect he became the source of eternal *salvation* for all who obey him."

(Hebrews 2:10; 5:8-9)

Just as man is destined to die once, and after that to face judgment, so Christ was sacrificed once to take away the sins of many people; and he will appear a second time, not to bear sin, but to bring *salvation* to those who are waiting for him.

(Hebrews 9:27-28)

The law is only a shadow of the good things that are coming—not the realities themselves. For this reason it can never, by the same sacrifices repeated endlessly year after year, make *perfect* those who draw near to worship... But when this priest [Jesus] had offered for all time one sacrifice for sins, he sat down at the right hand of God... by one sacrifice he has made *perfect* forever those who are being made holy."

(Hebrews 10:1, 12, 14)

Jesus, the perfect Son of the Father, the second person in the divine Trinity, the very *Logos* of God who was eternally pre-incarnate, the maker and sustainer of space and time, came to earth and lived a perfect life. He endured the pain and suffering of human life. Yet unlike anyone else, he maintained his perfect purity, never sinning. In doing so, he offered his own perfect self to be the perfect sacrifice for you and me, sinners who are unable to purify ourselves. The First Epistle of John clearly states how this happens:

This is the message we have heard from him and declare to you: God is light; in him there is no darkness at all... If we

155

> walk in the light, as he is in the light, we have fellowship with one another, and the blood of Jesus, his Son, *purifies* us from all sin… If we confess our sins, he is faithful and just and will forgive us our sins and *purify* us from all unrighteousness."
>
> (1 John 1:5, 7, 9)

It is crucial to note that it is not our walk in the light that purifies us, and neither is it our fellowship with one another. There is one and only one thing that can purify us from sin: the blood of the Son, Jesus Christ. As the Bible also says, "Without the shedding of blood there is no forgiveness" (Hebrews 9:22). In addition, the blood of Jesus cleanses us from all sin. All sin: past, present, future. Amazing, but true. This is surely the most fantastic fact of all time, the most important opportunity in all eternity.

Incredibly, many people will choose to reject this opportunity, just as the elder brother did in Jesus' parable of the prodigal son. This parable paints a terrific verbal picture of the offer of salvation. In this parable, the younger son is the best-known prodigal, but in the story there are actually two wayward sons. In fact, it is likely the main point of the parable is the elder son, not, as is so often interpreted, the younger. Jesus builds the whole parable to a climax not with the younger son's salvation, but as the father pleads with the elder son to come inside. The parable ends with the elder son upset, complaining, and petulantly choosing to remain outside the party. The listener naturally wonders, "What will the elder brother choose to do?" But Jesus does not provide the resolution. Instead, he leaves his audience hanging: did the elder son remain outside the party, or did he choose to humble himself, accept the father's love and enter the celebration?

This clever ending puts the onus on the listener: you are the elder brother. Others have already accepted his love and forgiveness, but what will you do? The father is now calling you to be saved and enter the feast with those who have been forgiven.

Friend, the party in heaven will go on with or without you. You can choose to reject the invitation, but that won't cancel the party. You can opt to disbelieve or even scoff at its likelihood, but that won't cause it to not exist. The party will happen, according to Jesus. There will be a banquet in heaven, a celebration the likes of which no one on earth has ever seen. The most important choice you will ever make, in all eternity, is this: will you be in or out? In other words, will you ask Jesus Christ to be your Lord and Savior, and will you trust in him alone for your eternal salvation?

Many of the readers of this book, I assume, have already done just that. I did it as a young teenager. Many have done it at an older age (one person in our church was baptized at 99 years old). If you have never done this, what possible reason could there be to choose to stay out of God's party—forever? Pray this prayer aloud:

> Lord God,
>> I admit I am not perfect and not pure.
>>> I have messed up tons of times in life,
>>> and I'm sure I will do so until the day I die.
>> Plus, there's nothing I can do to fix this or forgive myself.
>> I can't completely stop messing up or sinning,
>>> and I can't purify or become perfect on my own.
>> So I ask you, dear Father, to forgive my sins
>>> by the blood and in the name of your Son Jesus Christ.
>> I want to be a Christian,
>>> I repent of my past sins and prideful life,

and I confess my wayward actions.
I want to follow Jesus all the days of my life
I want to be a part of your Kingdom, now and forever.
I want in on the party!
In the name of Jesus,
the one and only Savior, Amen.

The Bible says the angels in heaven rejoice when one sinner repents, which means there is a party going on right now, in heaven, in your honor. Or, as Max Lucado puts it, there is "applause in heaven"[44] for your choice. Congratulations! You will be eternally grateful for this decision and this day. In the Bible, those who accepted this message were baptized (Acts 2:41), which is our public and symbolic identification with the death, burial and resurrection of Jesus. Find a Christ-centered, Bible-believing church, get baptized and get involved. Be a vital part of the family of God, not a visitor to church services once in a while.

When one becomes a Christian, in the imagery of the armor of God, that person puts on the helmet of salvation. To be more precise, God puts on us the helmet of salvation, since we cannot do this for ourselves. We cannot save ourselves, and we cannot even take credit for the decision to trust in and follow Christ. It's all from God, according to the Bible; it's all a part of his plan and the effective outworking of his will.

Protection for our thoughts

We have been discussing the second aspect of the functionality

44   Max Lucado, *The Applause of Heaven* (Nashville: Thomas Nelson, 1990), Chapter 18.

of a spiritual helmet, which we have said involves the protection of one's very soul survival. It provides and protects one's eternal salvation. But there is also another function of the helmet: it provides protection for one's mind and thoughts.

As we all know, the quality and content of our thoughts directly determine the quality and content of the rest of our lives. If our minds are filled with anxious thoughts, worries and fears, our lives will be dominated by dread. If our minds are filled with impure thoughts and images, we will be hard-pressed to not act these out in impure behaviors. If our minds are filled with anger, bitterness, or hatred, our remaining relationships will suffer. As the computer programming saying goes: GIGO—garbage in, garbage out.

This is why on *Thursday* we pray to *Think* within the helmet of salvation. Not only do both words begin with the digraph 'th' which differentiates Thursday from Tuesday, but 'think' pertains exactly to what goes on in our heads. We feel within our hearts, and sometimes even down to our guts. This is the reason the Greek word for 'compassion' is *splagchnizomai*, which is based on the root *splagchnon*, the word for intestines or bowels (the English 'spleen' is from this Greek root word). We think with our brains—or at least we are supposed to—and proper thinking leads to proper action.

It is for this reason that there are so many directives in the Bible to think correctly, and why we are warned that the pattern of our thoughts becomes the pattern of our lives. Solomon displayed both sides of this coin, when he wrote, "The thoughts of the righteous are right," and, "The thoughts of the wicked are an abomination" (Proverbs 12:5; 15:26, KJV). Plus, though we often mistakenly believe our thoughts are private, the Bible says otherwise: "The Lord knows the thoughts of man," and, "O Lord you have searched me and you know me…you perceive my thoughts from afar" (Psalm 94:11; 139:1-2).

Mind you—literally!—what we need is not merely more positive or possibility thinking. As we have already discussed earlier in this chapter, "The god of this world has blinded the minds of unbelievers" (2 Corinthians 4:4), and believers are to "put off your old self, which is being corrupted by its deceitful desires; to be made new in the attitude of your minds; and to put on the new self, created to be like God in true righteousness and holiness" (Ephesians 4:22-24). Yes, controlling the thoughts in one's mind is even difficult for mature Christians. The Apostle Paul, in his famous confessional to the Christians in Rome, said the habits and desires of our flesh battle against the principles of God in our mind (Romans 7:21-25). In other words, there is a battle being waged in our minds, which is why Paul instructed the Corinthians in his second letter:

> For though we live in the world, we do not wage war as the world does. The weapons we fight with are not the weapons of the world. On the contrary, they have divine power to demolish strongholds. We demolish arguments and every pretension that sets itself up against the knowledge of God, and we take captive every thought to make it obedient to Christ.
>
> (2 Corinthians 10:3-5)

Dear friend, have you learned how to take captive every thought, or do devilish and unclean thoughts still run un-captured and unrestrained, wreaking havoc in your mind and life?

How to take captive every thought

Paul was an expert at precise and philosophical thought, as we can see with his interaction with the philosophers in Athens in Acts 17, and in the sheer power of his logic and argumentation in his various letters to the churches. But Paul also knew that each person had to exercise control over his or her own mind; no one else can do that. He said to the Corinthians,

> For though we live in the world, we do not wage war as the world does. The weapons we fight with are not the weapons of the world. On the contrary, they have divine power to demolish strongholds. We demolish arguments and every pretension that sets itself up against the knowledge of God and we take captive every thought to make it obedient to Christ.
>
> (2 Corinthians 10:3-5)

But how do we take control of our thoughts; how do we win one the battlefield in our brains? His clearest appeal to control the content of our thoughts came in his letter to the Christians in Philippi:

> Do not be anxious about anything, but in everything, by prayer and petition, with thanksgiving, present your requests to God. And the peace of God, which transcends understanding, will guard your hearts and minds in Christ Jesus. Finally, brothers, whatever is true, whatever is noble, whatever is right, whatever is lovely, whatever is admirable—if anything is excellent or praiseworthy— think on these things.
>
> (Philippians 4:6-8)

Here is the best advice I know for gaining control of one's

thought-life, and the most practical way to implement what Paul taught in the afore mentioned passage: learn and practice *Christian meditation.*

Let me say a word here about what makes meditation Christian as opposed to most of what could be called Eastern meditation. As a kid growing up in the 70s, I heard about the Beatles and their temporary flirtation with Hinduism and Transcendental Meditation (TM). TM involved the mindless repetition of a meaningless word, a *mantra*, in order to disengage the brain and thus transcend this world of illusion. Frankly, the whole thing seemed escapist to me, and soured me on meditation. Our world desperately needed people to become more involved, not less, in order to fight injustice, abuse, etc. Meditation seemed to be a way of unplugging, rather than engaging and using, one's mind. It seemed the path to emptying, rather than filling, one's brain. It seemed to me the very opposite of what one should do. As the journalist G. K. Chesterton once said, "The object of opening the mind, as of opening the mouth, is to shut it again on something solid."[45]

I have since learned that Christian meditation does not empty one's mind; instead, it fills the mind with *Scripture*—with God's own words and thoughts. Biblical meditation is just that. We might even say that we are learning to think God's thoughts within our own brains. In this way, Christian meditation is not just trying harder, on our own power, to think better or with more purity. Instead, sincere Christian meditation is asking God to think his thoughts within us! It is asking God to put on us his helmet of salvation. Biblical meditation

---

45   G. K. Chesterton, *The Autobiography of G. K. Chesterton* (San Francisco: Ignatius Press, 2006), p. 217.

concentrates on specific passages of Scripture, as David described in Psalm 1:

> Blessed is the man
>> who does not walk in the counsel of the wicked,
>> or stand in the way of sinners
>> or sit in the seat of mockers.
> But his delight is in the law of the Lord,
>> and on his law he meditates day and night.
> He is like a tree planted by streams of water,
>> which yields its fruit in season
>> and whose leaf does not wither.
> Whatever he does prospers.
>
> (Psalm 1:1-3)

Here's another insight about Christian meditation: it is not repeating something silently and soundlessly in one's mind, as in eastern meditation. The Hebrew root word for meditation (used above in Psalm 1:2) is *haggah*, which literally means to mumble or even grumble. The second Psalm uses this Hebrew root word in its negative slant, "Why do the nations conspire, and the peoples plot in vain." (Psalm 2:1) The word translated *plot* in Psalm 2:1 is the same Hebrew word translated *meditate* in Psalm 1:2. How can this be?

Haggah is an onomatopoetic word, which means the pronunciation and the action sound similar, like the *buzz* of a fly, the *bark* of a dog, or the *bang* of a gun. My favorite onomatopoetic word is *spit*—say it slowly and you will hear every part of the action. In Hebrew, a person mumbling seems to be saying "*haggah-haggah-haggah*," just as, in English, a *mumbler* makes noises that sound similar to "mumble-mumble-mumble" and *grumble* sounds similar to "grumble-grumble-grumble." In other words, you can mumble positively or we can grumble negatively; there is good *haggah* and bad *haggah*.

Most of us do the latter. We constantly have negative conversations with ourselves going on in our minds, either worrying about things or replaying negative experiences in our lives.

> "I'm so worried about our finances. What if we lose our jobs…we could lose our home…we could end up homeless and on the streets…oh my, oh my…"

> "I'm worried about my kids…they keep making poor choices…they are hanging around with the wrong friends…I'm worried they may be hurt…they may get into trouble…may even get killed…"

> "I'm so angry at her. I can't believe she said that about me…or did such and such to me. It hurts so deeply. I wish someone would do the same to her, so she could feel how I feel…"

> "I'm so ashamed. I can't believe I did that…said that… thought that. I wish I could go back in time and do it differently. But I can't change the past, I really messed up, and now I'm stuck. Woe is me…"

These internal negative discussions with ourselves are notoriously hard to get rid of. Someone may have wronged us years—maybe even decades—ago, yet in the middle of the night we will start dwelling on that hurt. We toss and turn in our beds, trying to think about something else, count sheep, or even pray, but the old thoughts seem to persist and we lie awake for hours. What can we do?

The Bible's solution is to overcome poor thought patterns by repeating aloud, orally and quietly, God's thoughts on the matter. If you tend to worry over and over, try this: memorize a relevant Scripture and repeat—not just sub-vocally but vocally—the passage over and over. Let the words actually vibrate from your vocal chords, be formed in your mouth, and flow off your tongue. The negative scripts in our minds are sometimes so persistent that only real sounds can drown them out, only auditory vibrations can eclipse the silent destroyers in our heads.

If you are a worrier, memorize and *haggah* this Scripture, which we just quoted above. (Philippians 4:6-7 were the first verses I memorized as a new Christian, and almost 40 years later, they still are so very helpful in my prayer and meditation life.) This time, though, I don't want you to merely read these words silently in your brain. I want you to *haggah* these words from God, *haggah* his own words as your own. Pray these to God aloud:

> Don't worry about anything; instead, pray about everything with thanksgiving. And the peace of God, which surpasses all comprehension, shall keep your hearts and minds quiet and at rest as you trust in Christ Jesus.

If you are a grudge keeper, try these verses, or at least the last one:

> Do not let any unwholesome talk come out of your mouths, but only what is helpful for building others up according to their needs, that it may benefit those who listen. And do not grieve the Holy Spirit of God, with whom you were

sealed for the day of redemption. Get rid of all bitterness, rage and anger, brawling and slander, along with every form of malice. Be kind and compassionate to one another, forgiving each other, just as in Christ God forgave you.

(Ephesians 4:29-32)

No matter what I am struggling with, I have found great help and relief from meditating on Psalm 23:

> The LORD is my shepherd,
>> I shall not be in want.
>
> He makes me lie down in green pastures;
>> he leads me beside quiet waters.
>> he restores my soul;
>> he guides me in the paths of righteousness
>> For his name's sake.
>
> Even though I walk through the valley of the shadow of death,
>> I fear no evil, for you are with me;
>> your rod and your staff, they comfort me.
>
> You prepare a table before me in the presence of my enemies;
>> you have anointed my head with oil;
>> my cup overflows.
>
> Surely goodness and love
>> will follow me all the days of my life,
>> and I will dwell in the house of the LORD forever.

Haggah-ing Scripture, meditating on God's words, feels great, doesn't it? To do this successfully, we have to memorize various passages of the Bible, so we can call them to mind—whenever a disobedient or demonic thought needs to be taken captive. But here is where many Christians get lazy and balk: they claim to be unable to memorize Bible passages.

But I'm terrible at memorizing!

Don't give in to the excuse that I hear from many Christians: "I'm just not good at memorizing." Yes, you are. We all memorize facts about things that are important to us. Some people know the players on professional sports teams; others have memorized all the different car makes, models and years (and they can even differentiate them in traffic). Some parents remember every little comment their kids have said over the years. Some folks have memorized thousands of songs (quick: who sang "Dream On"? Right: it was Steven Tyler of *Aerosmith*); others thousands of recipes; others almost every iota of trivia (and they are champions in Jeopardy and Trivial Pursuit games). The human mind is remarkable. If you dig deep enough, I'm confident you'll find you are good at memorizing some category of details.

The secret, for many people, is to associate the verses with something they are good at memorizing. For instance, the musically-inclined often find Scripture is easy to memorize, if they tie it to a well-known tune. This trick can be used for other difficult memorization tasks. I memorized the Hebrew alphabet this way—to the tune of "Amazing Grace." During Hebrew class in seminary, when at my desk taking a test or doing an exercise, I often would hum "Amazing Grace," as I ran through the alphabet in my mind. My classmates probably thought I was spiritually deep; actually I was just trying to find a word in my dictionary. Even better, I still use this device to remember the Hebrew alphabet to this day.

For interior decorators, architects, realtors or even home-owners, one method many people use is to imagine a word or object from a verse in a successive room in a house. To memorize Psalm

23, for instance, you might imagine a shepherd who meets you at the front door. The shepherd leads you into the foyer, which has green grass and a water fountain; he then leads you down the hallway with pictures on walls of righteous people and the names of God; he walks you through the darkened living room that has a casket in the corner; etc.

Or a motor-head (in high school that's what we used to call people who loved and recognized different types of cars) might memorize Ephesians 4:29-32 by seeing a dozen cars lined up in a parking lot. The first one is a Mazda RX7 (M for "mouths" in verse 29a) with a driver yelling out the window; the second is a Honda (H for "helpful" in verse 29b) whose driver is encouraging and building up others around him; the next is a Gremlin (G is for grieve in verse 30; if you remember Gremlins, you will know this is a perfect fit) who is working on the engine and sealing the gaskets; and on and on. It sounds crazy, but it works.

The point is this: find something that you really love and know lots about, and tie verses to that imagery or content. Then, when you are tempted with unrighteousness⌐⌐—which is all the time—you can combat this mentally by repeating vocally or sub-vocally these Scriptures. The Bible calls this "praying without ceasing." The wandering monks in the Eastern Orthodox traditions did this by repeating "*Kyrie elision*" (Lord have mercy) over and over incessantly, thousand of times per day. Their testimony was that this type of *haggah* produced a harmony of spirit, soul and body so deep that even the beating of one's heart seemed to say "Kyrie elision," as did the inhales and exhales of one's breath.[46] Their claim was that their *bodies* began to pray![47]

Here is the antidote to worrying: worry is just talking with oneself about negative stuff, so the solution is two-fold. First, we must stop talking to ourselves and start talking to God (isn't it considered neurotic to talk to ourselves anyway?). If you worry a lot, just stop worring to yourself and start praying to God. You may become an instant expert at praying without ceasing. Second, replace that negative and devilish content with God's Word, the sword of the Spirit (which we will discuss in the next chapter). There you have it—an instant way to overcome worry and anxiety— a result of asking God to put on you his helmet of salvation.

Let's pray on the helmet of salvation

There is so much to pray about on Thursdays, so many Scriptures to meditate upon, so many true, noble, right, pure, lovely, admirable thoughts and people to ponder... well, we could end up praying all day, which again is what the Bible calls praying without ceasing. But let's restrict ourselves here to three model prayers. Pray these aloud for yourself, and then pray them again replacing the personal references with the different names of those you love, or slightly adapting the prayers as needed if your loved one is not yet a believer in Jesus.

And as we pray for God to enable us to think within the helmet of salvation, may God, in his power and grace, turn what usually is the

---

46 For more on the Jesus Prayer, read the *Philokalia* (Woodstock, Vermont: Skylight Paths Pub., 2008), Chapter 4.
47 Rock & Roll aficionados will recognize "Kyrie" as the title and theme of a 1985 Mr. Mister song.

devil's workshop into God's master-studio.

> Lord,
>> Thank you that, by your grace, I saw the light,
>>> I realized I was a sinner and an imperfect person,
>>> and I also grasped that heaven is a perfect place.
>> There's just no way I can save or forgive myself,
>>> and there's no way heaven will remain perfect if you
>>> let in 'pretty good' people like me.
>> I need to be purified, forgiven, and made perfect,
>>> and I know only Jesus can do that for me.
>> So I've asked Jesus Christ to be my Lord and Savior,
>>> and I know my assurance of being saved is
>>> firmly protected and kept by his power, not mine.
>> Thank you for the promise of salvation,
>>> that you have written my name
>>> in the Lamb's book of life,
>>> and that you are now preparing for me
>>> a mansion in Glory.
>> In Jesus' name, Amen

***

> Lord,
>> my mind is filled with
>>> worries, fears, and impure thoughts.
>> My mind is a mess.
>> Will you please come in and take control,
>>> and clean up the contents of my mind?
>> I ask you to put on me the helmet of salvation
>>> and teach me to think within that worldview.
>> Help me take captive every thought
>>> to make it obedient to Christ.
>> I ask you to help me not be conformed to this world,
>>> but please, dear Lord,

transform me by the renewing of my mind.
Then I will be able to test and approve what your will is,
    and I will not think more highly of myself than I ought.
In Jesus' name, Amen.

***

Lord,
    I want to learn to meditate upon your Word;
        I want to be filled with your thoughts;
        I want to be saturated in your ways;
        I want to be overflowing with your love.
I ask you to put your helmet of salvation upon me today
    and fill me with the very mind of Christ.
I don't want to be a positive-thinker,
    or a possibility-thinker,
    or a human-potential-thinker.
I want to be a Jesus-thinker,
    I want to think about Jesus all the time.
I want to be a Scripture-thinker,
    I want to be meditating upon your Word constantly.
I want you, O God, to think your thoughts inside me!
In Jesus' name, Amen

Chapter Seven

Friday: Fight with the Sword of the Spirit

"Thank God it's Friday!" is a well-known saying in our culture, so much so that it is even initialized in the name of a national restaurant chain (TGI Fridays). For many Americans, this is because the dreaded workweek is almost over, and the weekend is about to begin. Some people live for the weekends, and their midweek jobs are just a way to finance the weekend fun. In college, I worked for a welding supply company, and I was constantly amazed by some of these folks. They were miserable Monday through Thursday, and just when I thought they had no joy in them, they suddenly perked up on Friday. Their motto: *Get ready to par-tay!*

Actually, I love the saying, "Thank God it's Friday!" for three reasons. First, I love the reminder that it is God to whom we should direct our thanks. Second, I love whenever our culture mentions God. (I wonder: do militant atheists ever eat at TGI Fridays? Have they sued TGI Fridays on disestablishment grounds? Do they get upset at the reference to God in the company name or on the menu? Does that spoil their appetite?)

But the third, and in my mind the most meaningful reason I thank God for Fridays, has to do with the armor of God: Friday begins with the letter 'F,' which is my mnemonic device reminding me to 'Fight with the sword of the Spirit."

Let's begin in prayer:

Lord,
>   We come to you on Fridays,
>>   so very thankful for your mercy, grace and love.
>   We are overwhelmed with how good you are to us,
>>   and overjoyed everyday to walk personally with you.
>   People around us look forward to the weekend
>>   to party with drugs and alcohol,
>>   to anesthetize themselves for a short while,
>>   to create a temporary, mock version of happiness.
>   But we want to be filled with your Spirit because
>>   we know you are the true and unending source
>>   of lasting joy, peace, and contentment.
>   Plus, we know you are preparing a feast for us in heaven,
>>   a celebration that will go on forever,
>>   a party that will far surpass all earthly parties.
>   We ask that you put on us and our loved ones, today,
>>   your very own armor, O God,
>>   so we can be protected from the evil one,
>>   whose goal is to keep us out of your eternal party.
>   We are not powerful enough to defend ourselves from him,
>>   not wise enough to even recognize all of his schemes.
>   Protect us this day, we pray,
>   In the name of Jesus, Amen.

An offensive weapon, at last!

Even first-time Bible readers quickly realize the first five pieces of the armor of God are designed for defense, not offense. They are protective devices only, and not able to inflict much, if any, damage on an opponent (one could conceivably throw a shoe, or hit with a shield or helmet, but the pieces of armor were not designed for those actions).

Roman soldiers had an offensive weapon, which Paul did not mention: the *pilum*, a spear with an iron head and a strong, thick staff. The spear was about seven feet in length, and was positioned to injure incoming soldiers or even horses. It was used in concert with the large shield, which Paul did include. With spears lowered and shields forming a protective wall, a Roman regiment could repel an attacking army, and could even advance slowly but steadily.

Instead of the *pilum*, though, Paul instructed the believers to "Take...the sword (*machaira*) of the Spirit." The Roman *machaira* was just under two feet in length, double-edged and kept extremely sharp. Its point came to what Wilbur Fields called "quite an obtuse angle," which gave the sword added strength, while also allowing it to penetrate enemy armor or flesh more efficiently. A Roman soldier's *machaira* was made in Spain, and usually was worn on the right side, hanging from a sword belt (*baldric*).[48]

The sword was important as a weapon for hand-to-hand combat. If the *pilum* was unsuccessful at defeating the enemy a pace or two out, and if the *thureos* was not able to keep the enemy at bay, the *machaira* had to do the job.

But in the spiritual arena in our fight against the darkness of evil, our one and only offensive weapon, Paul specifies, is the Word

---

48 Fields, p. 191.

of God. This means there is power in the Word of God. Have you discovered this yet? There is power in the Word of God to guide our lives, power to direct us, power to help us, and power to prevent us from making mistakes. But most of all, there is power to injure the enemy, and power to inflict damage to the kingdom of darkness.

Once again, our society just cannot comprehend this. Our cultural elites tend to look down at the Bible, which Christians claim is the written Word of God. They think the Bible is merely a collection of ancient, irrelevant writings. Instead, believers maintain that God has revealed himself to us in the Bible, both who he is and how he wants us to live. The Bible, if we follow it, provides a moral rock upon which we can live our lives, a solid foundation for ourselves and also our family, friendships, marriage, community, nation—everything.

Historically speaking, the Bible was the moral rock upon which our nation was founded. This information may be overlooked in public classrooms today, but that does not change the facts. Our forefathers based this country on biblical principles. George Washington said, "It is impossible to righteously govern the world without God and the Bible." (If George Washington were alive and said this today, would he be sued by the ACLU?) Andrew Jackson said, in reference to the Bible, "That book, sir, is the rock upon which our republic rests." (If our republic seems shaky today, maybe it is because the rock has been taken away, and the republic now rests on nothing but the hot air and whims of personal opinion.) Ronald Reagan, just a few years ago, said, "Within the covers of one single book, the Bible, are all the answers to all the problems that face us today—if only we would read and believe."

The problem is just that. Many people own a copy of the Bible, but they neither read it nor believe it. They certainly don't know its contents. As George Gallup said, "We live in a country of biblical illiterates,"[49] which wasn't true 200, or 100 years ago. Two centuries ago, people were taught to read by reading the Bible, they learned morality from the stories in the Bible, and they were ethically trained by the Ten Commandments from the Bible.

Today, people are biblically illiterate in our culture. In a recent survey Americans were asked,

- "Who preached the Sermon on the Mount"? Four out of 10 people could not name who preached the Sermon on the Mount.
- "Name one of the Gospels." A majority of citizens could not do so.
- "What is the reason for Easter?" Only three out of 10 teenagers knew the correct answer was the resurrection of Christ.

Biblical literacy is even in decline among Christians. In one survey Christians were asked,

- "Is the book of Thomas in the Bible?" 22% said yes.
- "Is the book of Jonah in the Bible?" 27% said no.
- "What was the birthplace of Jesus?" 16% said Jerusalem, while another 8% said Nazareth.

---

49 George Gallup and JimCastelli, *The People's Religion: American Faith in the 90s* (New York: Macmillian, 1989), p. 60.

Jesus' use of the sword of the Spirit

But why are reading, studying, and even memorizing the Bible important? There are many benefits, which could be listed, but the one pertinent to this book is the Bible's value in spiritual warfare. As we can see in the life of Jesus himself, when attacked by the evil one, there is no better weapon available to defeat him.

The greatest example of this, of course, is the temptation of Jesus in the wilderness. How did Jesus, as our model and exemplar, deal with temptation?

His response to the devil's first temptation, to turn stones into bread in order to satisfy his hunger, is very illuminating.

> Jesus answered, "It is written: 'Man does not live by bread alone, but on every word that comes from the mouth of God.'"
>
> (Matthew 4:4)

Here Jesus modeled not only that the Word of God can be used as a weapon during times of temptation, but he chose the Scripture, Deuteronomy 8:3, which described God as a God who speaks. In one quote, Jesus masterfully affirmed the Word of God with the Word of God. Now, I realize this next bit of dialogue is not recorded in the text, but my hunch is the devil said back, probably under his breath, "Shoot, I hate it when he does that." The score read: Jesus 1; Satan 0.

The devil is a quick learner, so he snatched an old play out of his playbook. I imagine the devil thought to himself, "I know. If he is going to follow Scripture so much, I'll misquote Scripture. I'll misquote what God said, which is my oldest trick of the trade. This is the strategy I used against the woman in the Garden of Eden when I asked her, 'Has God really said?' With Jesus I'll have to be more subtle, so I will just slightly twist and misapply God's Word."

He then led Jesus to Jerusalem for the second temptation, and had him stand on the highest point of the temple. Then the devil said to Jesus,

> If you are the Son of God, throw yourself down. For it is written, "He will command his angels concerning you, and they will lift you up in their hands, so that you will not strike your foot against a stone."
>
> (Matthew 4:6)

Amazingly, the devil here quoted from Psalm 91:11-12, which means he used the sword of the Spirit against Jesus. This reveals that the devil knows the Bible too, though he misapplied it. The lesson is obvious: it is not enough to know the Scriptures; they can be known and still misused. Proper use of the Bible is not to merely quote the verses which will serve our own purposes; instead, we must understand and obey the Scriptures in their appropriate sense. Jesus alluded to this in his answer, thereby successfully defending himself from temptation.

> It is also written: "Do not put the Lord your God to the test."
>
> (Matthew 4:7)

What an incredible moment! Jesus met the sword thrust of Satan with a parry of his own by quoting Scripture, specifically Deuteronomy 6:16. In my spiritual imagination, this encounter appears to me as a swordfight between two massive, ancient gladiators. Or, to summon a modern parallel, this was like two Jedi knights from the

178

Star Wars movies, fighting with light sabers. One light saber was blue while the other was red, corresponding to the good versus the evil side of the Force. In the same way that light was used for either good or evil, so too the sword of the Spirit can be used or misused.

But the battle between Jesus and Satan is no myth or legend; it was an actual event that took place in time and history—and, in a sense, also above and beyond time and history. In this battle, the swords were not made of earthly metal or futuristic light, but they were potent nonetheless. So here we have, in this wilderness outside Jerusalem, Jesus and Satan swinging their supernatural swords at one another. The preternatural sparks must have been flying; the cloud of unseen witnesses must have been fascinated in rapt attention. It was a moment of archetypal warfare, a preliminary round in the cosmic bout that would end with the destruction of the old heaven and earth, and the creation of the new (Revelation 20).

But at this point, the devil is not defeated; he merely loses another point, so the score read: Jesus 2; Satan 0.

I bet the devil whispered, "Shoot, there he did it again. He's really good at this."

In the third and final temptation, the devil pulled out all the stops. He took Jesus to a very high mountain and showed him all the kingdoms of the world, along with their splendor, and said,

> All this I will give to you if you will bow down and worship me.
>
> (Matthew 4:9)

But Jesus said in response,

> Away from me, Satan! For it is written, "Worship the Lord your God, and serve him only."
>
> > (Matthew 4:10)

I just love that answer. Jesus, in effect, said to Satan, "No, no, no. You can't misquote and misapply Scripture and get away with it, because Scripture is consistent. God never contradicts himself. Therefore, because the Bible says elsewhere that we should only worship God, you are clearly misusing and misquoting the Word of God."

The score read: Jesus 3; Satan 0. With this, the devil gave up. The battle was over; Jesus was just too well armed. Matthew simply records,

> Then the devil left him, and angels came and attended him.
>
> > (Matthew 4:11)

In all three temptations, Jesus answered, "It is written." Dear friend, this is how we are to fight against evil. This is the way we wage war against darkness: we turn on the light of God's Word by using Scripture in a specific application. Jesus could have chosen to argue with the devil, but he did not. Instead, he used his powerful offensive weapon, the sword of the Spirit.

Before we move on, I have a question for you: do you think Jesus had a copy of the Scriptures with him in the wilderness? Matthew records for us that Jesus had no food during his 40 days in the wilderness (Matthew 4:2). Do you think he had a bunch of scrolls that he was carrying around with him?

Of course not. But then a second question arises: how was he able to quote these passages? The only sensible explanation is that Jesus had previously memorized them. He had hidden God's Word in his heart, so he was ready and mightily equipped when the moment of battle came. His sword was well-oiled and finely sharpened. He was ready for spiritual warfare.

This is the power of God's Word. As we privately study it week in and week out, as we go to church and listen to the Word of God preached, as we go to a home Bible study and devote ourselves to the Apostles' teaching (Acts 2:42), and as we daily read the Scriptures to our children in their beds, God plants his Word in our hearts. Then, when the moment of battle comes, God will bring these Scriptures to mind, through the power of the Spirit, just when we need them.

When Jesus was in need, he often turned to the Scriptures. His reliance on the Scriptures was profound, and was especially apparent during his times of suffering and distress. For instance, when Jesus was on the cross and just at the brink of death, Matthew recorded,

> About the ninth hour Jesus cried out in a loud voice, *"Eloi, Eloi, lama sabachthani?"* which means, "My God, my God, why have you forsaken me?"
>
> (Matthew 27:46)

Most Christians are aware that Jesus, there on the cross, was quoting David from Psalm 22:1. Jesus had been raised in the synagogue, memorizing and praying the Psalms, so in his time of need, spoke a prayer he learned from them. In the most excruciating (literally!) moment of his life, the Scriptures gave voice to his deepest feelings. Jesus expressed his question to God and articulated his loneliness—both in God's own words! I am in awe at such honesty, such brilliance, and such self-control.

The Word of God in the Old Testament

Paul specifically identifies the sword of the Spirit as "the word of God" in Ephesians 6:17. The concept of the 'Word of God,' though, did not originate in the New Testament. This foundational concept also filled the Old Testament as it revealed a God who speaks and who revealed himself in and through speech. God is a God who uses words.[50] Because God is inherently powerful, his words, therefore, are also inherently powerful.

This is especially evident in the first five books of the Bible, known in Hebrew as *Torah*.[51] The Spirit of God, even in Genesis 1, is a God who not only created a well-ordered world, but did so through the vehicle of speech. God's movement was a linguistic movement.[52] He acted in a verbal way. There is no reference in Genesis 1 to any metaphor such as the hands of God in shaping and designing creation, but instead, only the voice of God was noted. The Genesis author repeatedly wrote, "And God said."[53] Amazingly, this is all that was

---

50   Nicholas Wolterstorff in *Divine Discourse*, gives an extensive, philosophical answer to the question: What does it mean to claim that God speaks? Furthermore, is an intelligent person in today's world entitled to claim that God has spoken to him or her? For Wolterstorff, 'speaking' is not synonymous with 'communication' (p. 32), it does not necessitate the use of words (p. 38), and it is not merely "expressing knowledge." (p. 35) Instead, for Wolterstorff "to speak is not, as such, to express one's inner self but to take up a normative stance in the public domain." (p. 93) Therefore, "God must act if God is to speak" (p. 117), and "divine discourse…requires direct intervention by God in the affairs of human history: and contemporary science provides us no good reason for thinking that such intervention does not occur." (p. 129) He concludes: "So yes; it is possible for an intelligent adult of the modern Western world to be entitled to believe that God has spoken to him or her." Nicholas Wolterstorff, *Divine Discourse: Philosophical Reflections on the Claim that God Speaks* (Cambridge: Cambridge University Press, 1995).
51   In seminary I was taught, contrary to common usage, that *Torah* does not take a definite article. In honor of my professor, I follow that Hebraic usage in this book.
52   William Yarchin, Ph.D, "The Spirituality of Scripture and Its Proclamation," a Doctor of Ministry Course at the Haggard School of Theology, Azusa Pacific University, January 7, 2002.
53   Genesis 1:3; 1:6; 1:9; 1:14; 1:20 & 1:24.

needed for creation to occur, for the heavens and earth to come into existence. Since God is inherently powerful, his words have the power to create reality from nothing. The mere Word of God was able to create light, sky, dry ground, seas, and every living thing.

This God who spoke all reality and created beings into existence, continued to speak throughout *Torah* and the rest of the Hebrew Scriptures. God spoke to Adam and Eve; to Cain and Abel; to Noah, Abraham, Isaac, Jacob, and Joseph; and then supremely to Moses. The Bible disclosed that God is a God who speaks and *Torah*, from the Hebrew root word which means simply "teach," is God teaching Israel how to be his special people. *Torah* contains God's instructions regarding who and what the Israelites were to be. In fact, the main point of *Torah* is neither the creation stories nor the Exodus deliverance. Instead, the central message is the Word, or teaching of God, which shapes Israel's new identity.

This concept of God as the speaking God, whose words have an inherent power, is continued in the Prophets, which follow *Torah* in the Hebrew canon. Both the Former Prophets (the historical books such as 1 and 2 Samuel, 1 and 2 Kings, etc.) and the Latter Prophets (the prophets such as Isaiah, Jeremiah, Ezekiel, etc.) again reveal God to be a speaking God. This emphasis is prominent right away in Samuel, in which the narrative began with the barren Hannah praying to God, and the promise from Eli that God has listened to her prayer. She gave birth to a boy, named Samuel, whom she dedicated to the Lord. God soon revealed himself to Samuel as the speaking God. He called to Samuel in the night, and, under Eli's instruction, Samuel simply said to the Lord, "Speak, for your servant is listening" 1 Samuel 3:10.

This historical event is an archetypal illustration of exactly who God is and whom his people are to be. God is the God who speaks, and his people are primarily to be listeners.

Immediately following the Samuel narratives are the stories about the kings of Israel, beginning with Saul, David, and Solomon. These too can be seen as an ongoing illustration of the importance of listening to the speaking God. When a king listens to God and obeys, the nation prospers. Conversely, when a king fails to listen to God and disobeys, the nation suffers.

During the reigns of the latter kings, God raised up prophets not only to communicate his Word but also to illustrate that he was still the God who speaks. Prophecy in Israel was primarily an oral phenomenon. A prophet was always, by definition, a speaker sent to speak to someone else, but not meant to speak his or her own words. Instead, a prophet was simply to speak what had been spoken to him or her by God. A prophet could not speak until spoken to.

Therefore, though the book of Jeremiah began with "The words of Jeremiah, son of Hilkiah, one of the priests at Anathoth in the territory of Benjamin" (Jeremiah 1:1), it quickly added from where his words came. Before Jeremiah could speak, God first had to speak to him. That is why the second verse showed that God took the initiative. It is the power of God's Word that gave Jeremiah words to say: "The word of the Lord came to him in the thirteenth year of the reign of Josiah son of Amon king of Judah" (Jeremiah 1:2). In the same way, the book of Ezekiel begins with, "The word of the Lord came to Ezekiel the priest" (Ezekiel 1:3). Hosea begins with, "The word of the Lord that came to Hosea son of Beeri" (Hosea 1:1). Joel begins with, "The word of the Lord that came to Joel son of Pethuel" (Joel 1:1).

The power inherent in the Word of God was invested not only in these oral events, but also derivatively when these oral events were written down. Interestingly, though the prophets themselves did not literally write the books that bear their names, there were scribes who wrote down what they said, and these writings themselves came to be seen as having inherent divine power.[54] God's words are so powerful that they retain their power whether uttered by God, or by representatives of God such as Moses, kings, and the prophets, or even when they are rendered in written form. The Word of God even retains its power when read off a page.[55]

But why does God speak? Why does God choose to move linguistically? There are probably many possible answers, since the Scriptures themselves do not provide a definitive one. The answer I like best is that of Eugene Peterson, who notes that only language can produce the development of *object permanence*. Without language, we would not develop the belief that God exists independently from ourselves. As a result, the times that God is silent or seems absent do not lead us to believe that God no longer exists. Peterson goes on to

---

54   An example of this can be found in Jeremiah 36:1-32.

55   Many people today are confused when they first learn about the writing, editing and redacting apparent in the Bible. Some even decide such details call into question whether the Bible can truly be God's Word. (For instance, see Bart Ehrman, *Misquoting Jesus*, New York: HarperCollins, 2005.) My opinion on the matter is that writing and even editing are not contrary to the idea of inspiration, but can certainly be led by the Spirit of God also. In fact, a case could be made that even in the writing down and editing of the historical events or prophetic words, the Spirit of God was still moving and active. The final written product is no less the Word of God than the first time the prophecy was spoken, even though the two might be expressed from different viewpoints or for different purposes. If we believe that the written Scriptures are the true Word of God, then we must see the scribes as inspired as well. We can say, then, that the prophets are not the only ones who were inspired. The Spirit of God continues to move linguistically throughout history and God continues to be a God who speaks and who shapes his people through speech in a variety of forms.

say,

> Language is the primary means we have of acquiring 'object permanence.' The discovery that there is a word 'ball' that refers to that round green fuzzy object that rolled under the dry sink, is a key to dealing with the reality of 'things unseen.' Words attest to the reality and distinctiveness of people and things and events that are outside the realm of my sensory experience. As I develop facility in words, my world expands; before long I am inhabiting remote centuries, dealing with faraway continents, having conversations with men and women in the cemeteries. So it is not surprising that God, who is 'far beyond what we can ask or think' should deal with us by means of language. God speaks. For Christians, basic spirituality is not a noun, God, but also a verb, *Said* (or *Says*)."[56]

The Word of God is self-installing

One of my favorite Scriptures about the power of God's Word is found in Hebrews 4:12:

> For the word of God is living and active. Sharper than any double-edged sword, it penetrates even to dividing soul and spirit, joints and marrow; it judges the thoughts and attitudes of the heart.

We see, in this Bible passage, the firm belief that God not only has spoken but continues to speak, for the Word of God is characterized as living and active. The word "living" in Greek was from the root *zao*, which was commonly used to refer not only to living beings, but

---

56   Eugene Peterson, *Subversive Spirituality* (Grand Rapids: Eerdmans, 1994, 1997), p. 23.

also to God as the living God. Just as God is living and as humans and other creatures are living, so too the author of Hebrews claimed the Word of God is living. The Scriptures are breathing beings, as are the animals and humans. In other words, the Spirit of God is still moving through the written Scriptures.[57] This is why Paul calls the *machaira* the sword of the *Spirit*.

In addition, Hebrews 4:12 also described the Word of God as "active." This word in Greek was from the root *energes* from which evolved our English word "energy," and which can be variously translated "effective," "active," or "powerful."[58] The Greek word itself was derived from another Greek phrase *en ergo einai*,[59] which can be translated "to be at work" or "to set at work." According to Kittel and Friedrick, the word *energes*, from the time of Aristotle, meant "active."[60]

---

57 Eugene Person argues persuasively that God's Word is living because it is always meant to be heard. God both wills that we listen and provides for this. "Happily, we are not left to our own devices in these difficulties. The God who wills to reveal himself to us in word also wills our listening and provides for it. St. John tells us that the word of God that brings creation into being and salvation into action became flesh in Jesus, the Christ. Jesus is the word of God. One large dimension of St. John's Gospel shows Jesus bringing men and women into conversation with God—no longer merely reading the Scriptures, at which many of them were quite adept, but listening to *God*, which they hardly guessed was possible. At no place in St. John's Gospel is the word of God simply there—carved in stone, painted on a sign, printed in a book. The word is always sound: words spoken and heard, questioned and answered, rejected and obeyed, and, finally, prayed. Christians in the early church were immersed in these conversations and it changed the way they read the Scriptures: now it was all voice. They heard Jesus speaking off of every page of the Scriptures. When they preached and taught they did not expound texts, they preached 'Jesus'—a living person with a living voice. They were not 'reading in' Jesus to their Scriptures, they were *listening* as if for the first time and hearing that word that was in the beginning with God and through whom all things were made and whom they had seen and touched, now hearing the word of God made alive for them in the resurrection. The dead body of Jesus was alive, so was the dead letter of Moses." Eugene Peterson, *Working the Angles*, (Grand Rapids, MI: Eerdmans, 1987), p. 72.
58 Bauer, Arndt, Gingrich, *A Greek/English Lexicon of the New Testament and Other Early Christian Literature* (Chicago: University of Chicago Press, 1957), p. 265.
59 Gerhard Kittel and Gerhard Friedrick. *Theological Dictionary of the New Testament*, translator and editor, Geoffrey W. Bromiley (Grand Rapids, MI. William B. Eerdman's Publishing Company, 1964), Vol. II, p. 652.
60 *Ibid.*

This is a dynamic understanding of the Word of God. By using the word *energes*, Paul asserted there is an inherent power, within the Word itself, which is causal. As William L. Lane noted in his commentary on Hebrews,

> The description of God's Word as…'living and effective,' signifies that it is performative; it possesses the power to effect its own utterance. Performatives, by definition, commit the speaker to stand by his words.[61]

This idea that the Word of God has the power to effect its own utterance is exactly what we have been discussing: the power inherent in the Word of God. Scripture possesses the power not only to speak God's truth, but also to bring about the actual occurrence of God's will.

This is an incredibly marvelous truth, one which I hold near and dear to my heart, though I realize it is well-hidden in the above technical discussion of word origins and meanings. An illustration from the world of computer technology might be helpful in grasping this central truth. The Word of God is inherently powerful, much like most computer programs today are *self-installing*. Do you remember the tortuous days of DOS, in which we laboriously had to install computer software on our own? Fortunately, those days are now behind us. Today, we merely put a new program disc in a computer (or click 'download' on the internet), and the program wonderfully self-installs (much to the delight of non-techies, like myself).

In a similar fashion, "active" means that the Word of God is

---

61   William L. Lane, *Hebrews 1-8, Word Biblical Commentary*, volume 47a, (Dallas: Word Books, publisher, 1991), p. 103.

self-installing. Just reading and meditating on the Scriptures alone releases the inherent power of the Word of God, which will gradually self-install the will and wisdom of God into our lives. This is why it is so crucial that Christians and churches alike return to the practice of regular Scripture reading. Because the Word of God is "living and active," there is value in the simple public and private reading of Scripture, even though no interpretation or application is given, and may not seem profitable at the time. The Word of God does not need to be made relevant; once it self-installs, it will effect its own relevance.

The same root *energes* is also found in Paul's letter to the Christians in Thessalonica:

> And we also thank God continually because, when you received the word of God, which you heard from us, you accepted it not as the word of men, but as it actually is, the word of God, which is *at work* in you who believe.
> (1 Thessalonians 2:13; emphasis added)

Again, we see that the early Christian community understood God to be a God who speaks, not only in the accepted and authoritative Scriptures, but now through his spokespeople: the apostles, preachers and teachers. The Spirit of God is moving and still is at work in the lives of the believers.

To bring this full circle, let me point out that this idea, God is at work through his Word, harkens back to the very beginning of the Bible. In the book of Genesis, the Septuagint translated God's finished "work" with the Greek root *erga* (Genesis 2:2), which was the root from which *energes* was derived. In other words, just as God was at work in creation through the power of his Word, so God today continues to be at work through the power that is still inherent in the Word of God, whether written, read or spoken.

This is one reason (among many) to attend church regularly and stay awake during the sermon (I say that not out of ill-will towards those that nod off habitually during my sermons). As a preaching pastor, I believe it is God's Word that changes lives, not my words about God's Word. Because of this, my commitment as a pastor is to provide solid teaching from the Scriptures to our church family. One of the top goals in our church is that parishioners, of all ages, learn the Bible. Every week the Bible is planted into our hearts, with the confidence that over time it will grow and bear fruit in our lives.

To this end, we relentlessly study the Bible and give out hundreds of free Bibles each month (sometimes each week). Other churches may be more clever in their sermonic content and lesson series, but, as I often say to new families and individuals, "If you get involved in our church and stick with it for a few years, you will learn the Bible." This also is why we do not put the main verses of the Bible passage we are studying up on the video screens, which, I have found, actually makes it easier for people to leave their Bibles at home. Instead, we encourage all believers to bring a Bible with them to church in order that they can turn, in their own Bible, to the relevant page. In this way, each of us can grow in our ability to handle Scripture, the sword of the Spirit, just as a soldier learns to use a sword by constant practice. The Bible is still the most powerful, ultimate weapon available to Christians today against the darkness of evil, but we must become familiar with it in order to use it properly in the heat of battle.

The sum of all this is that God wants to do his work in our lives, and he accomplishes that through his Word by the power of his Spirit. Plus, there is even more: the Bible gives this powerful and self-installing Word of God a name—Jesus.

Jesus is the Word

There are many famous first lines in literature. Some think Melville's *Moby Dick* is the best: "Call me Ishmael." Others believe Charles Dickens deserves the honor for his first sentence in *A Tale of Two Cities*: "It was the best of times; it was the worst of times."

For me, the prize goes to the first verse in the book of John: "In the beginning was the Word, and the Word was with God, and the Word was God" (John 1:1). In this verse, John remarkably echoes the first book of Genesis, thus drawing in his Hebrew audience, while at the same time alluding to the *logos* of ancient philosophy, thus pulling in his Greek readers. But he affects a cataclysmic change, a paradigm shift of massive proportions, when he reaches the punch line in verse 14:

> And the Word became flesh and dwelt among us. We have seen his glory, the glory of the One and Only, who came from the Father, full of grace and truth.
>
> (John 1:14)

In the monotheistic, Hebrew culture of John's day, this was revolutionary. According to the Old Testament, God selected the Jewish people to be his own chosen race. God did this not for preferential treatment (Really, would you like to be treated as the Hebrews have been for 4,000 years?), but so he could slowly develop a place in which he could fully appear and reveal himself. In the book of Genesis, God spoke to Abraham, the Patriarch of the future Hebrew race, as a disembodied voice in a vision (Genesis 15:1). In Exodus, God appeared to Moses from within the burning bush (Exodus 3:4), and later filled the Sanctuary in the wilderness with his own glorious presence (Exodus 40:34).

In John 1:14, God brought these elements together. The speaking, appearing, glorious God finally descended to earth in a human body and "made his dwelling among us," which in Greek literally means, he "tabernacled" among us. The Old Testament Tabernacle in the wilderness has now been superseded in the very body of Jesus: he is the living, breathing, walking tabernacle of God. Plus, as the book of Hebrews so brilliantly explains, every main function of both the mobile Tabernacle and the immobile Temple were shadows of the reality which would take place in Jesus himself. Jesus is the atoning sacrifice, he is the high priest, he is the bread, he is the light, he is the mercy seat, he is the glory, and he is the Word. In a fascinating display of typology over 1500 years before his life, the Old Testament provided all of the vocabulary of faith by which Jesus could be fully understood.

In Jesus, the Word of God became flesh. So, once again, we see that to put on the armor of God is to put on Christ. When we take up the Word of God as the sword of the Spirit, we do not become Bible-bashers who hit people over the head (whether emotionally or physically) with the Bible. No, to take up the Word of God as a sword is to take up Jesus as an offensive weapon with which we can fight off the evil one. This imagery appears especially vivid in the book of Revelation, in which Jesus is depicted with a sword coming out of his mouth (Revelation 1:16; 2:12, 16) with which he will fight the nations and armies that follow the beast (19:15, 21).

Which, of course, is exactly what Paul said in Ephesians 6: the Word of God is an effective weapon to use against the forces of evil in this world.

The Bible is meant to be applied specifically

It is time now for a surprise, because in Greek there are two words for 'word.' We have been talking about the Word of God, the *logos*, which appears in both John 1:1, "In the beginning was the Word (*logos*), and the Word was with God and the Word was God," and Hebrews 4:12, "The word (*logos*) of God is living and active, sharper than any double-edged sword."

But—surprise—the Greek term for 'word' which Paul uses in the phrase "Take up...the sword of the Spirit which is the word of God" is not *logos*, it is the Greek word *rhema*. *Logos* is the Word of God in its entirety, its totality, in its all-sufficiency. The Word of God, Jesus himself, is sufficient for anything we may need and for any situation we may face. *Rhema*, in contrast, represents the Word of God in its specific application. What is the difference? It is very slight, but, simply put, *rhema* doesn't refer to the Word of God in its entirety, rather it signifies the Word of God as it applies to particular situations.

To be honest, I must point out that the words are often used almost interchangeably. In the Gospel of Luke, Peter said to Jesus, "At thy word (*rhema*) I will let down the net" (Luke 5:5 KJV), while the Centurion said to Jesus, "But say the word (*logos*), and my servant will be healed" (Luke 7:7). In 1 Peter, the terms appear in consecutive verses:

> For you have been born again, not of perishable seed, but of imperishable, through the living and enduring word (*rhema*) of God. For,
> "All men are like grass,
>   and all their glory is like the flowers of the field;
> the grass withers and the flowers fail,
>   but the word (logos) of the Lord stands forever.
> (1 Peter 1:23-25)

Though *logos* and *rhema*, at times, appear to be synonyms, it is often the case that the *rhema* of God is also used in a slightly different and more specific sense than *logos* is used.[62] *Rhema* is when God wants to use his Word, Holy Scripture, and he wants to speak that Word into our lives to help us face specific challenges. This is what Jesus did. When facing the devil, Jesus used the Word of God, the *rhema*, in that he used specific Scriptures to fight the enemy's precise attacks. This is exactly what the Scriptures are meant do in our lives. God wants Scripture to come alive for us, to be a tool to help us as we daily face the clear-cut challenges of our opponent.

This has happened many times in my life. One of the clearest examples of this was an incident involving our church and our local city council. Several years ago we acquired an undeveloped parcel of

---

62 The relationship between *logos* and *rhema* might be better termed a metonym or a synecdoche, rather a synonym, since ultimately *logos* is the cause of all cases of *rhema*.

land upon which we hoped to build our future church home. Some local businesses did not want us on that particular piece of property, and they encouraged the council to prevent us from building by enacting an "emergency zoning ordinance revision."

Our church prayed fervently about this, and met with city officials who, thankfully, assured us both the law and logic were on our side. We presented our case at the city council meeting, and were flabbergasted when the council voted 5-0 against us. The law was changed right out from under us. We had hoped to build a church home, to have a place for our church family and our community outreach programs, yet they pulled the rug out completely from under us. I was devastated. After the vote was taken, the joy left the room as if a giant had punctured the atmosphere like a balloon with an oversized pin. We were all deflated.

Suddenly, I felt God wanted me to say something. With a prayer in my heart, "Please God, give me inspiration," I jumped to my feet and said, "Mr. Mayor, before you take an intermission, I have something to say on behalf of our church."

Inside, I was praying. Then a Scripture came to mind so I prayed, "God, your Word says you will give us 'the words to speak when we stand before the magistrates and councils.' God, if that ever applies—it's now. I'm standing here before the council, so give me wisdom."

But nothing came. No inspiration. Zero. Zip. I fumbled around for a few seconds, and then proceeded to stall by thanking the council members. I was hoping that God would send the needed inspiration during my stall tactic. Still, nothing came.

In hindsight, it is clear to me that God, in fact, did give me wisdom and inspiration. After thanking each council and city staff member, I again thanked them collectively for the time they spent with us, for the advice they gave us, and for the direction they provided us that night. Still feeling inspiration-less, I said,

"Bottom line we just want to thank you, and we want you to know that we're looking forward to working with you in the future."

They probably had never before been thanked for a 5-0 negative vote. I believe God inspired that. As I went to sit down, and the mayor said, "Don't sit down."

I jumped to my feet and he said, "Rick, we have never met a church like yours before. We want you in our town." That night they put in motion a long process that culminated with us moving our current property. We not only took "possession of the land' (Joshua 1:11), but it is one of the finest pieces of church property anywhere in the nation.

God was involved, for in that story was a *rhema* of God. God's Word was specific in its application. The *rhema*, I believe, was not when I said "Thank you." The *rhema* was the Scripture which related perfectly to my predicament, and through which God gave me the needed confidence to move ahead in that specific context. The *rhema* was, the Holy Spirit will give us the words to speak when we stand before "the magistrates and councils" (Luke 12:11-12; KJV).

The Scripture, applied in an appropriate and timely fashion, was the *rhema*. My thankfulness, I believe, was certainly a result of the inspiration and the prompting of the Spirit, but I don't consider that to have been a *rhema* of God. This is why: some Christians, in my opinion, go off in the deep end in this area. They claim a *rhema* is anytime one feels that God has given specific direction, which is tantamount to whenever one feels inspired by God.

These well-meaning Christians often say, "God said to me," "God spoke to me," or "I have a word from the Lord."

As a pastor I am very cautious about this. God certainly inspires and leads people today, but I refuse to equate promptings and personal inspiration with the authority of Scripture, which happens when one calls such experiences a word from God. I believe this can be very dangerous. In the worst case scenarios, megalomaniacal leaders like Jim Jones and David Koresh claimed to have a word from God, and their followers were tragically led astray.

This happens, in a much less dangerous fashion, even in evangelical Christian circles. For example, I have seen this several times in singles ministries in churches. I remember a woman who said to me, "Rick, a man just told me God spoke to him that I'm supposed to marry him. What am I supposed to say back? There's no way I would ever want to marry him."

I responded, "Tell him that God can speak to you also, and so far he definitely hasn't. I would never recommend marriage unless both people feel strongly led by the Lord to tie the knot."

In the end, not only did they not get married, but his 'proposal' alienated her from him. His comment actually pushed the woman away, rather than drew her interest towards the man. She said, "I want a man who wants me, and not one who just claims to be obeying God. Why do some Christian guys have to hide behind God like that?"

As a pastor I encourage believers to use phrases such as "God told me…" very cautiously. I may say that God spoke when referring to how a Scripture perfectly applied to a certain situation in my life. But when I say, "God is leading me" or "I feel God's Spirit guiding us," I am very sure to not add, "This is a word from the Lord." There is a major difference between *rhema* of Scripture and a personal sense of prompting.

How to find the Word (rhema) of God in everyday life

When we begin to live in the power of God's Word and utilize the sword of the Spirit, the *rhema*, in our daily battles, we experience a wonderful difference in our lives. The way to do this is simple. Simply read, reflect, and pray about a portion of the Bible everyday. When we do this faithfully and regularly, an astonishing thing occurs: the passages we read in the Bible seem to line up with the needs in our daily lives. The challenges we will face later in the day are mysteriously covered in that morning's Bible reading section.

Here are a couple of helpful hints that I have learned in my years of reading the Bible. First, don't try to read too much. If we try to read too much, it's difficult to see the nuggets and diamonds because we have covered too much ground. If we read the Bible like we are trying to set reading records, we may find we get through it quickly, but have nothing from God, no *rhema*, for the day.

Second, when reading a passage of Scripture, proceed slowly and pause often. Pause on sentences as they strike you; linger over arresting phrases or even single words. Maybe this was the purpose behind the Hebrew word *Selah*, found seventy times in the Psalms. *Selah* may have been a musical term of uncertain meaning, but many scholars think it signified that readers or singers were to pause at that moment. In Psalm 3:1-6, for instance, David writes:

> O Lord, how many are my foes!
>> How many rise up against me!
> Many are saying of me,
>> "God will not deliver him."
>>>> *Selah*
>
> But you are a shield around me, O Lord;
>> you bestow glory on me and lift up my head.
> To the Lord I cry aloud,
>> and he answers me from his holy hill.
>>>> *Selah*
>
> I will lie down and sleep;
>> I wake again, because the Lord sustains me.
> I will not fear the tens of thousands
>> drawn up against me on every side.

A pause at the correct moment is essential to music—just as it is crucial in the spiritual life. In the midst of David's troubles, which were numerous, each *Selah* allowed David to ponder. Likewise, *Selah* breaks our train of thought, precisely because it is an indefinable word. It forces the reader to pause, which lets the meaning of the previous phrase settle in.

When you read the Bible for daily guidance from God, take your time. A propitious pause allows God the space needed to drive home his message. With each pause, pray for God to speak to you through that section. Simply pray, "God, what do you want me to think about today, based on this? What word do you have for me today?" The devotional masters called this type of Bible reading *Lectio Divina*, which is Latin for 'Divine Reading."

Third, select one word, phrase or verse as a thought for the day. For years, I wrote these daily thoughts on scraps of paper or old business cards, which I would put in my pocket and carry with me during the day. Today one could use a smart-phone or iPad; I often send myself a text message to keep the *rhema* on my mind for the day.

I am often astonished to find what I write down in the morning often has an application that day. The Scripture I write down provides exactly the guidance or reassurance I need later. The shocking part is not that God is involved—it is that I am continually shocked. I know I should not be surprised that God knows in advance what I need each day, but when I experience his provision, it never ceases to amaze me. his mercies indeed are new every morning (Lamentations 3:22-23).

Fourth, don't worry if part of the passage doesn't make sense to you. We don't have to understand all of it in order to be blessed. This may surprise you, but be assured that even when bible professors or seasoned pastors study the Bible, they don't understand everything. I certainly don't. I believe that none of us will understand the Bible in its totality until we are on the other side of Glory. Why? Because our brains just are not big enough. So settle for modesty in your devotional time; read and try to understand a little bit at a time.

My last piece of advice is for parents: don't neglect to read the Bible with your children. Start with a children's Bible when they are young. Make sure it has lots of pictures, and tells the stories concisely and in simple terms. My kids loved this. Every night we would gather on the couch to read a short section. Over time, we even developed our own game based on the Bible. My wife or I would ask a question such as:

"Who built a big boat?" and they would yell in response, "Noah!"

"Who was the strongest man that ever lived?" "Samson!"

Over the years the questions became harder and harder, but it was still fun.

"Who were thrown into the fiery furnace?" "Shadrach, Meshach and Abednego." (Amazingly, kids can get details like this right, just as they can memorize the names of different dinosaur species or the four Teenage Mutant Ninja Turtles.)

"How do you spell Nebuchadnezzar?" (Just kidding. We never made this seem like school or homework.)

Here's the benefit: somehow, in God's gracious economy, when we daily read the Bible and pray, God's Word gets into the very fabric of our being. We can't add it up according to scientific, measurable methods, but God's ways are not our ways (Isaiah 55:8). Over the months and weeks, years and decades, God's Word gradually saturates our souls, eventually bringing God's *shalom*, his wholeness and peace, to our lives.

The same thing also happens in our kids' *nephesh*, their souls. That's why it is so important for parents to read Bible stories with their children, to encourage them to memorize Scripture, get them into Sunday School programs, and then in the teenage years into youth groups. Why? So God's Word is stored slowly, but surely, in their hearts. They won't remember all those Scripture stories, and they won't remember all their memory verses. Nonetheless, over time there is a residual effect. God brings great wisdom, purpose and peace into their lives.

Thank God it's Friday!

I just love Fridays, because on Fridays, I get to pray the sword of the Spirit on those I love. It doesn't matter whether I am out jogging, or driving my car, or getting up from or lying down in my bed. Whatever I am doing, I think, "Okay, today is Friday. Friday begins with the letter 'F,' which is my reminder to Fight with the sword of the Spirit.

And so I pray, on Fridays, that my loved ones would be strong in the Word of God. Parents and grandparents, think about this for a moment. Would you like your children to grow up to be strong in the Word of God? What a terrific way to help put God's Word in their hearts. What a fantastic way to help them through all of the storms of life, storms that may come even after we are dead and gone. Singles, would you like your friends to be strong in the Word of God? Pastors, would you like this for your congregants? How about for your neighbors, co-workers, or government leaders? I pray this whether they are believers or not—that they would come to value and follow the Word of God.

Personally, I start off praying for my wife, and then my kids. For my children, I pray for them somewhat along these lines. (Join me by praying this aloud, with your kids in mind. If you are not a parent, pray this for someone else who is dear to you.)

> Lord,
>> My kids today will step into the battle zone;
>>> they will have the flaming arrows of the enemy
>>> launched at them all day long.
>> The enemy is relentless, and his only desire

for them is to kill and destroy.

Selah

I pray that you would put on them your full armor, O God,
    so they can take their stand against the evil one.
Today I especially pray you help them
    take up the sword of the Spirit,
    which is the Word of God.
Help them become strong in your mighty Word.

Selah

I pray you would plant your Word in their hearts
    like a mustard seed that will grow large and healthy.
I pray they come to firmly believe
    your Word is trustworthy, logical, and factual.
Help them believe from the top of their heads
    to the tips of their toes,
    that trusting and obeying your Word
    is the smartest thing they will ever do.
I pray your Word becomes, in their minds and hearts,
    their daily source for wisdom and guidance.

Selah

In the name of the Word himself, Jesus, Amen.

For my precious wife, I pray for her to become more and more a woman of God's Word. I pray for our marriage, that our marriage would more and more reflect God's Word. I pray for our church that we would more and more be a church of the Word. I pray for the people in our community, state, country and world, that their spiritual eyes would be opened, and they would see the wisdom and truth about God's Word. I love Fridays!

Chapter Eight

Saturday: Steadfastly Pray in the Spirit

It's Saturday, and we have come to the end of our weekly adventure. Of course, the word *Saturday* is not a Christian term; it is named after Saturn, the Greek god of agriculture.[63] Nevertheless, we can redeem the day for the Lord by starting off in prayer, as we have learned to do each day of the week.

> Lord,
>> What a privilege it is to come to you in prayer.
>> What an honor it is to speak with you personally,
>>> even the ability to do so is an unfathomable wonder.
>> I come to you because I am in a battle zone,
>>> as are those I love.
>> The evil one is hurling his flaming arrows at us,
>>> and we need your protection.
>> Please put on us your very own armor, O God,
>>> clothe us with Christ!

---

63 Because the traditional names of the days of the week were named by the Romans after the gods who ruled the planets, as they knew them two millennia ago, and the astrological power those planets supposedly exerted on humans, the Quakers to this day chose to call them by their numerical order: First Day, Second Day, etc., so the Seventh Day is called just that. See Daniel Boorstin, *The Discoverers*, New York: Vintage Books, 1983, p. 15.

Teach us today how to draw close to you in prayer,
In Jesus' name, Amen.

The Sabbath Day

The biblical name for the last day of the week, in contrast, is Sabbath, or *Shabbat* in Hebrew. An early form of the word *Shabbat* first appears in Genesis 2, at the end of God's creation week:

> Thus the heavens and the earth were completed in all their vast array. By the seventh day God had finished the work he had been doing; so on the seventh (*shebee-ee*) day he rested (*shebot*) from all his work. And God blessed the seventh day and made it holy, because on it he rested from all the work of creating that he had done.
>
> (Genesis 2:1-3)

These few verses are very interesting in Hebrew because there is a slight play on words between 'seven' and 'rest,' since both words sound very similar in Hebrew. The second verse says, if you will pardon my mixed translation: "He *shebot*(ed) on the *shebee-ee*(th) day." In fact, both words are derivatives of the same Hebrew root *shaba*, which meant to be 'complete.' From this notion of completeness or fullness came the concept that seven was the perfect or complete number, and thus the seventh day was the completion of the week.

Is seven a lucky number or a godly number?

From this moment on, the word 'seven' takes on special meaning in the Bible. It is considered not only the symbol of perfection and completion, but also of divinity. After the exodus from Egypt, the Hebrews were to eat unleavened bread for seven days on certain occasions (Exodus 12:15; 34:18), seven lamps were to be placed on the lampstand in the Tabernacle (symbolized today by the Jewish *menorah*, the seven-branched candlestick used in both the Tabernacle and the Temple; see Exodus 25:37 and 2 Chronicles 4:7), and the priests were to sprinkle sacrificial blood seven times on the altar (Leviticus 4:6), etc. This reverence for the number seven carries over into the New Testament, for instance, in Jesus' teaching on forgiveness (a disciple is to forgive not just seven times, which Peter thought was the perfect amount, but 77 times; Matthew 18:22), and the use of the number in his parables (Mark 12:20; Luke 11:26). Seven was also the number of deacons the apostles chose for the new church in Jerusalem (Acts 6:3), and it appears quite often in Revelation, where the number seven is mentioned over 50 times (for instance, the Lamb who was slain is pictured with "seven eyes and seven horns"; Revelation 5:6).

Most Bible readers know that seven is a symbolic number in the Bible, but I'll bet most haven't learned this fact: the word seven was also the way in which persons in the Old Testament *swore*. When King Abimelech asked Abraham to agree to the treaty at Beersheba by taking a solemn oath, Abraham said, literally in Hebrew, "I *seven* it" (Genesis 21:24). Most English translations render this verse, "I swear it" thereby retaining the idiomatic intention, but losing the colorful etymological meaning. Likewise, when God declared an oath to the kings of Judah, he said, "If you do not obey these commands, I *seven* myself that this palace will become a ruin (Jeremiah 22:5). The idea here was that this single oath was as clearly the truth as if one were to repeat oneself seven times.

Maybe this is where the number seven gained its status as a lucky number. In the Bible it seemed to be a number God preferred, which trickled down into our modern, western culture. It is interesting to note that seven is not considered a lucky number in some cultures (such as the Chinese[64]), which are not descended from Judeo-Christian roots, as is western civilization. Even the name Saturday, since for the Romans it was the day governed by the planet Saturn, was a day of evil portent. As the historian Daniel Boorstin wrote in his bestseller, *The Discoverers*,

> Among the Romans, Saturn's Day, or Saturday, was a day of evil omen when all tasks were ill-started, a day when battles should not be fought, nor journeys begun. No prudent person would want to risk the mishaps that Saturn might bring. According to Tacticus, the Sabbath was observed in honor of Saturn because "of the seven stars which rule human affairs Saturn has the highest sphere and the chief power."[65]

Boorstin incorrectly suggests it was partially from this etiology that a seven-day week evolved. Let me point out the Romans had eight days in their week. Saturn may have been designated the seventh because of the seven planets, but that merely placed Saturn's Day after the sixth day; it did not delineate a limit of seven days to a week. In fact, Boorstin even admits the seven day week was adopted by Roman

---

64 In Chinese culture, the even numbers are usually considered lucky and the odd ones unlucky. Seven is known as the ghostly number and can even refer to death. The seventh month on the Chinese calendar is even called 'the ghost month,' during which the spirits and ghosts of the dead are believed to be released from hell and are free to roam the earth.

There also is an English limerick that paints seven as an unlucky number:
"One means anger, two means mirth, three a wedding, four a birth, five is heaven, six is hell, but seven's the very day of the devil himself."

65 Boorstin, p. 14.

culture only in the early third century,[66] which reveals it was the result of the influence made by Jews and Christians in the Roman world.

For the Romans, Saturday was not the final day of the week, nor was it a lucky day. It was a day of "evil omen," so it certainly was not the source of the notion of lucky number seven. Instead, that seems to have Judeo-Christian roots. It is my opinion that those who call for a "lucky seven," when they roll the dice or pull the one-arm bandits, are dimly reflecting a Judeo-Christian heritage whether they know it or not; when Frank Sinatra talked in his songs of 'sevens,' he was reflecting the Bible that he so often derided. The influence of the Bible shows up in the most unlikely places.

The most amazing impact of the number seven

So seven is an amazing number in the Bible, and conveys several important meanings in addition to its numerical meaning. But the most revolutionary, historical fact about the number seven, based on the Genesis account of God's creation of the heavens and the earth, is that time began to be measured in seven day weeks.

Today, the concept that time is divided into weeks containing seven days is a world-wide belief. But this was not the case in the ancient world. Most cultures followed a lunar calendar, which turned over roughly every 30 days.[67] The Babylonians followed a calendar based on the number six, which was also the basis of their numerical system. The Romans had an 8-day week, whereas the Greeks apparently had no week. As Boorstin noted, "Around the world,

---

66 Boorstin, p. 13.
67 "So long as man marked his life only by the cycles of nature—the changing seasons, the waxing or waning moon—he remained a prisoner of nature." Boorstin, p. 12.

people have found at least fifteen different ways, in bunches of 5 to 10 days each, of clustering their days together."[68] Boorstin even points out that the Babylonian word *sabattu* "appears to have survived from the years the Jews were in Babylonian captivity."[69]

So why did the Hebrews decide seven days would comprise a week? It was a highly improbable choice: seven did not divide nicely into the lunar month, and neither did it divide evenly into the solar year. There really was only one reason they chose to include only seven days in a week: revelation. God worked for six days and then rested on the seventh, so the basic unit of days per week must be seven. The fourth of the Ten Commandments specified, "Observe the Sabbath day by keeping it holy, as the Lord your God has commanded you. Six days you shall labor and do all your work, but the seventh day is a Sabbath to the lord your God. On that day you shall not do any work…" (Deuteronomy 5:12). In addition, the Sabbath became a memorial of the Jew's exodus from Egypt, which signified their liberation from slavery (Deuteronomy 5:15).

A massive paradigm shift: it is good to rest!

So why seven? The number does not seem to be derived from any structural relation to the cycles of nature or the laws of the universe. God could have chosen the fifth day, and our calendars would have been simpler. Instead, the significance of seven goes back to the etymology with which we began this chapter: the relation of seven (*shebee-ee*) to rest (*shebot*). Here is the Copernican revolution,

68   Boorstin, p.13.
69   Boorstin, p.14.

the massive paradigm shift the Hebrews brought to the world: humans should *rest* at regular intervals.

It's okay to relax, to put your feet up, and take a break once in a while.

God modeled this in his own creation activity, and he wanted humans to follow suit. But humans are notorious workaholics, and even when they have enough, they tend to want more. So God codified the Sabbath, and asked humans to make it holy—by resting. In the early days of Sabbath-keeping, this had nothing to do with going to church or even worshipping.[70] Yes, you read that correctly: Sabbath originally did not involve any acts of worship. Read Exodus 20:8-11 and Deuteronomy 5:12-15 again, and you will notice the only thing God instructs us to do on the Sabbath is rest. In fact, the regular cycle of weekly worship had not even been established yet. There is no record in the Bible that the Patriarchs worshipped God weekly; instead, they seemed to do so on a rather rare and haphazard schedule. Plus, God gave this command to Moses decades before the Jews had a sanctuary around which they could worship, and long before the sacrificial system was developed. The early Bible characters did not go to the Temple or to the synagogue on the Sabbath, and they were not even instructed to worship or pray. They were only told to rest!

In human history before this, people worked 24/7 (sort of

---

70 Christians are sometimes confused over whether the proper day for worship is Saturday or Sunday, and whether worshipping on Sunday is breaking the Sabbath commandment of Exodus 20:8-11. This issue merits a full study, but my response, in a nutshell, is that Christians worship every day of the week, rather than just one, because every day is theologically a day of rest for followers of Christ. Theologically, Christians gather for worship at the first of the week not to celebrate the Sabbath, but to celebrate his reversal of the need to earn our own rest. We start and then conduct our whole week at rest in Christ. Practically, the need to have a full day of rest is still of great value for all human beings, so Christians, in our workaholic culture, would be wise to rest one day a week. But this has no relation to a day set apart for worship.

like workaholics—most of us—do now). In pre-industrial cultures, there was always more work to do. Free people and children, slaves and animals, everyone worked. Unless one was royalty, one worked nonstop, from sunup until sundown, all life long. This is one reason life expectancy was so short, in addition to disease and war: people simply wore out earlier; the nonstop hard work took its toll.

As Thomas Cahill writes in *The Gift of The Jews,*

> No ancient society before the Jews had a day of rest. The God who made the universe and rested bids us do the same, calling us to a weekly restoration of prayer, study, and recreation (or re-creation)... The Sabbath is surely one of the simplest and sanest recommendations any god has ever made; and those who live without such septimanal punctuation are emptier and less resourceful.[71]

Sabbath was a revolutionary invention in the ancient world, as a God-blessed, restful Saturday also would be in our modern world, if we would practice it. There is no need to get legalistic, like the Jewish leaders did in the time of Jesus, about what constitutes work. Instead, do what comes naturally—even our dogs know how to do this. Take it easy, take a breather, take a load off. As my kids would say, "Chill, Dad."

---

71 Thomas Cahill, *The Gift of the Jews* (New York: Doubleday, 1998), p. 144. Cahill also waxes eloquently in his discussion of the Sabbath on how the innovation of a day of rest paved the way for education and even the notion of the universal right to education:

"In this study (or Talmud), we have the beginnings of what Nahum Sarna has called 'the universal duty of continuous self-education,' Israel being the first human society to so value education and the first to envision it as a universal pursuit—and a democratic obligation that those in power must safeguard on behalf of those in their employ. The connections to both freedom and creativity lie just beneath the surface of this commandment: leisure is appropriate to a free people, and this people so recently free find themselves quickly establishing this quiet weekly celebration of their freedom; leisure is the necessary ground of creativity, and a free people are free to imitate the creativity of God."

211

Let's thank God for this:

> What a great God you are, Lord Almighty;
>> How good you are to us, your followers and children.
> No idols ever were said to command people to rest,
>> not those of the Canaanites, Egyptians, or Philistines.
> You alone truly desire our best interests,
>> and command us in ways that are healthy for us.
> What a loving heavenly Father you are.
> In Jesus' name, Amen.

Saturday: a day to rest in God by resting in prayer

To this point we have learned how to ask God to put on us the six pieces of the armor of God, as described by the Apostle Paul to the Ephesian church. As I mentioned in Chapter One, once I realized the value of praying on the armor rather than merely trying harder to produce those qualities on my own, I began praying the armor of God with fervor. How exciting it was praying the armor of God on my wife, our three kids, and our extended family. Once I got going, I naturally included our church, close friends, the nation and world in my prayers of protection. I thoroughly enjoyed praying in this manner, but it took a long time. So I began to pray one piece of armor per day, and soon noticed that the six pieces left Saturday open, so to speak. What was I to pray about on Saturday?

I went back to Ephesians 6 and noticed how Paul ended his discussion about the armor of God. The passage did not end with the 'sword of the Spirit,' as we can tell from the word that follows 'Spirit' in Greek: "and." Paul provided the conjunction 'and' to connect the armor of God with this important instruction:

And pray in the Spirit on all occasions with all kinds of prayers and requests. With this in mind, be alert and always keep on praying for all the saints. Pray for me, that whenever I open my mouth, words may be given me so that I will fearlessly make known the mystery of the gospel, for which I am an ambassador in chains. Pray that I may declare it fearlessly, as I should.

(Ephesians 6:18-20)

In other words, Paul says the last step in putting on the armor of God is: *keep praying about it.* Use all kinds of prayers, all sorts of requests, and pray for all types of people—including him. After we have prayed for God to put on us his own armor, we are to rest and put matters solidly in his hands. Will we be sufficiently protected from the evil one? Will any of the darts or arrows get through to injure us? Well, it's not our concern any longer. We trust God to take care of all things: "He who began a good work in you will carry it on to completion until the day of Christ Jesus" (Philippians 1:6). We do all this through prayer.

What is prayer, after all? Christian prayer is not a strategy we execute to curry favor. It is not the way we punch our spiritual timecard in order to earn his blessings. It is not a way to prove to God our sincerity, nor is it a way we earn rewards from him. It is not a duty we perform. It is not work at all. Exactly.

Prayer is the ultimate form of resting in God.

In prayer, we give over to God our needs, our desires, and our wishes. We ask for his will, not our own, to be done in our lives. We trust that his way is best, and we rest in faith that our heavenly Father will take care of us, both now and forevermore. We entrust our health, our well being, and our very lives into his safe keeping. Consider, for instance, the spiritual and psychological rest that is conveyed by these biblical prayers (pray them as you read):

> To you, O Lord, I lift up my soul;
> > In you I trust, O my God.
> Do not let me be put to shame,
> > nor let my enemies triumph over me.
>
> (Psalm 25:1-2)

> Many are the woes of the wicked,
> > but the Lord's unfailing love
> > > surrounds the man who trusts in him.
>
> (Psalm 32:10)

The following verses remind us that, since horses and chariots were ancient implements of war, we cannot, even with the armor of God, trust solely in the armor. As we learn to pray on the armor of God, we must never forget this important fact. (See also Psalm 44:6-7)

> Some trust in chariots and horses
> > but we trust in the name of the Lord our God.
>
> (Psalm 20:7)

For those who struggle with fear and worry, these two verses are especially comforting:

> When I am afraid,
> > I will trust in you.
> In God, whose word I praise,
> > in God I trust;
> > > I will not be afraid.
>
> (Psalm 56:3-4)

214

These prayers are in the Bible for our edification, but also for our use. We can pray them for ourselves and for others. This is, I believe, what Paul referred to in Ephesians 6:18: "Pray…with all kinds of prayers and requests," and in Ephesians 5:18-19: "Be filled with the Spirit. Speak to one another with psalms, hymns and spiritual songs. Sing and make music in your heart to the Lord." The book of Psalms is filled with every type of prayer imaginable: praise, supplication, lamentation, thanksgiving, etc. For centuries, this is why Psalms has been called the prayer-book of the church, and why monastic communities pray through the Psalms on a regular basis. In the church in which I serve, this is what we do on the elder board. We pray through the Psalms, allowing God's Word to supply the topics for prayer, and his own words to supply the verbiage. Every time we meet, we begin our meetings in prayer—on our knees—praying aloud and in one accord the next Psalm. Over the years, we have often remarked how timely a specific Psalm was to the needs of our church that very day. When we are led by God's Spirit and are persistent in prayer, God's Word is truly relevant.

Why don't we pause here and give this a try? I suggest you go back a few paragraphs and pray the psalms that I quoted. Pray them aloud, first for yourself. This works perfectly when the psalmist wrote with first-person pronouns. An example of this would be: "In you I trust" or "I will not be afraid." Then pray those Scriptures again, this time adjusting them to fit the names and pronouns of your loved ones. For instance, let's try the last Scripture quoted above. Read it aloud as a prayer for yourself to God.

When I am afraid,
    I will trust in you.
In God, whose word I praise,
    in God I trust;
        I will not be afraid.

(Psalm 56:3-4)

Next, insert the name of a loved one and adjust the pronouns and verbs accordingly. For instance, I pray for my wife,

Dear Lord,
    When Amy is afraid,
        let her trust in you.
    In God, whose word she praises,
        in God she trusts;
        Amy will not be afraid.
    In Jesus' name, Amen.

Now pause and do the same for your other friends or family members. If you choose to visualize this, imagine the nail-pierced hands of Jesus are reaching out, cupped together as if to receive something from you. Imagine your loved one in your hands, and as you pray this prayer, open your hands and visualize the image of your loved one falling into the secure hands of Jesus.

Fearfulness is a common trait among humans. I'm always amazed that even small children are often full of fear, even to the point of having nightmares and night tremors. What can parents do to help their little treasures find peace? Prayer is the answer. Pray with them for God's peace to fill their hearts and minds, the peace of God that passes understanding (Philippians 4:7). When my kids were young and afraid, I placed a hand on their chests and would pray a prayer of peace. In addition, my wife placed a tape recorder (an ancient device!) in their rooms and played kid's praise music as they fell asleep. The last input into their brains was peaceful and full of Scripture. If they awoke in the middle of the night due to a bad dream, we taught them to just turn the tape over and hit the play button.

I have given this advice to many parents who were concerned about the bad dreams that were terrorizing their children. So far, this little suggestion has always worked wonders. Of course, it is God who works this wonder, through the prayers of protection by the parents, and through the power of the Word of God, even when contained in commercialized children's music.

Scriptures to pray for rest

There are hundreds of other such verses in the Bible, Scriptures we can pray to God to express our desire to trust in him rather than in ourselves, to have faith, and to *rest* in him. I love the passages in the Bible that talk about this rest, and I love praying them as protection for those I love. As you read the following verses, pray them aloud for someone in your life who is troubled, and who is especially in need of spiritual rest:

> He (substitute a name here) who dwells
> in the shelter of the Most High
> will rest in the shadow of the Almighty.
> I (substitute the same name here) will say of the Lord,
> "He is my refuge and my fortress,
> my God, in whom I trust."
>
> (Psalm 91:1-2)

217

In that day the Root of Jesse will stand as a banner for the peoples (substitute a name here); the nations (substitute the name here again) will rally to him, and his place of rest will be glorious."

(Isaiah 11:10)

Come to me, all you (substitute a name here) who are (is) weary and burdened, and I will give you rest. Take my yoke upon you and learn from me, for I am gentle and humble in heart, and you (substitute the name here) will find rest for your souls. For my yoke is easy and my burden is light.

(Matthew 11:28-30)

My favorite Scripture to pray, when I am troubled and my spirit is not at rest, is David's magnificent prayer recorded in Psalm 23 (we already prayed this on Thursday, but it is a helpful prayer for every day of the week). It never fails to bring a peace and restfulness to my mind, heart and soul. Pray it out loud for yourself and those you love, by name and one at a time, as you read this moving prayer:

The LORD is my shepherd,   •
   I shall not be in want.
He makes me lie down in green pastures'
   he leads me beside quiet waters'
   he restores my soul.
He guides me in the paths of righteousness
   for his name's sake.
Even though I walk through the valley of the shadow of death,
   I fear no evil, for you are with me;
   your rod and your staff, they comfort me.
You prepare a table before me in the presence of my enemies,
   you have anointed my head with oil;

my cup overflows.
Surely goodness and love
    will follow me all the days of my life,
    and I will dwell in the house of the LORD forever.

(Psalm 23:1-6)

Jesus: the High Priest of prayer

Here is a common question that concerns many believers: how can we be sure our prayers are heard and received by God?

Fortunately, the Bible says that Jesus serves as our High Priest. This is especially helpful when, as they say, the going gets tough; it is wonderfully comforting, when we get bogged down by temptations and suffering. The book of Hebrews encouraged believers to not give up because Jesus, as our High Priest, is just the help we need. As you read the following passage, I'm sure you already know the drill: first pray this for yourself, aloud and by name. Then pray it again, substituting the name and pronouns appropriate to a loved one:

> Since we have (I have… or Noah has…) such a great High Priest, even Jesus the Son of God, let us (me… etc.) hold firmly to the faith we profess. For we do not have a high priest who is unable to sympathize with our weaknesses, but we have one who has been tempted in every way, just as we are—yet was without sin. Let us then approach the throne of grace with confidence, so that we may receive mercy and find grace to help us in our time of need.
>
> (Hebrews 4:14-16)

Another reason Jesus is the perfect High Priest of prayer is that he provided the perfect model for his followers to imitate. Very early in Mark's Gospel—Chapter One, in fact—the writer records this little

219

incident: "Very early in the morning, while it was still dark, Jesus got up, left the house and went off to a solitary place, where he prayed" (Mark 1:35). Clearly, prayer was very important to Jesus. He was willing to give up sleep and go to great lengths to find privacy for prayer.

As an aside, this Scripture was very formational in my early spiritual development. I desperately wanted to grow as a person of prayer, and I was determined to follow Jesus in this regard. So I set my alarm clock to an early hour, got up before dawn, and retreated for a concentrated time of prayer. During one period of my life, I even endeavored to pray for an hour a day. Many times, on those cold, dark mornings, I would repeat to myself, "If Jesus could do it while he was on earth, then maybe Jesus in me can do it now." After many such mornings, I became a morning person! In addition, this little prayer has helped me innumerable times as I have faced challenges and difficult situations; I was armed because I knew my great High Priest had successfully navigated those rapids before.

When fasting, I prayed, "Since Jesus could fast for forty days, then maybe Jesus in me can help me fast for one or a few days." When tempted, I prayed, "If Jesus could be tempted yet sin not, then maybe Jesus in me can do the same now." When I have had people attack me and accuse me falsely, I was able to pray, "If Jesus behaved like a lamb before his shearers was silent, then maybe Jesus in me can help me keep my mouth shut now." How hard those moments were, yet how helpful it was to know I had a High Priest who was able to not only sympathize with me, but was living within and willing to empower me. Once again we are reminded of the tremendous truth that it is not we who live, but Christ who lives in us (Galatians 2:20).

Plus, Jesus was the all-time expert at prayer. Luke records that Jesus prayed at his baptism: "As he was praying, heaven was opened and the Holy Spirit descended on him in bodily form like a dove" (Luke 3:21-22). He often isolated himself for prayer: "Jesus often withdrew to lonely places and prayed" (Luke 5:16). On at least one occasion Jesus spent an entire night in prayer: "Jesus went out to a mountainside to pray, and spent the night praying to God" (Luke 6:12). He also would take time to pray in private, even when his disciples were with him (Luke 9:18), and sometimes he took a few of them on special prayer hikes: "Jesus took Peter, John and James with him and went up onto a mountain to pray..." (Luke 9:28).

No wonder the only skill the disciples asked Jesus to teach them was, "Lord, teach us to pray" (Luke 11:1). He even prayed in agony on the night of his arrest (Luke 22:39-46), and he prayed while on the cross that the Father would forgive those who had just crucified him (Luke 23:34). What an incredible man of prayer, and what a wonderful model for us to follow. Apparently, prayer was not something he did occasionally or only when needed. Instead, prayer was his *modus operandi*, his strategy for living; we might even say prayer was his battle plan for the combat he would wage against the evil enemy on this battleground called earth.

Jesus repeatedly used this plan

When beginning his ministry, Jesus prayed. When confronting a big decision, he prayed. When in trouble, Jesus prayed. After big problems, he prayed. In the Garden of Gethsemane, Jesus prayed the same thing three times (Matthew 26:39-44). It seems as if Jesus prayed all the time; he was in constant communication with his Father.

One time Jesus' friend Lazarus of Bethany died and was buried, and Jesus came belatedly to the town. Lazarus' family and friends had already been four days in mourning, and Jesus wept when he saw their pain. He instructed the mourners,

> "Take away the stone."
>
> "But Lord," said Martha, the sister of the dead man, "by this time there is a bad odor, for he has been there four days."
>
> Then Jesus said, "Did I not tell you that if you believed, you would see the glory of God?"
>
> So they took away the stone. Then Jesus looked up and said, "Father, I thank you that you have heard me. I knew that you always hear me, but I said this for the benefit of the people standing here, that they may believe you sent me."
>
> When he said this, Jesus called out in a loud voice, "Lazarus, come out!" The dead man came out, his hands and feet wrapped with strips of linen, and a cloth around his face.
>
> Jesus said to them, "Take off the grave clothes and let him go."
>
> (John 11:39-44)

This incident reveals that Jesus felt he was in constant communication with his heavenly Father, because Jesus said to God,

"I knew that you always hear me." What would it be like to know that God always is involved in our lives, always hears our thoughts and prayers, and always will do what is best if we invite him to do so?

Later, Jesus prayed in a way that again reflected his constant communion with God, his intimacy and oneness with the Father.

> I pray also for those who will believe in me through their message, that all of them may be one, Father, just as you are in me and I am in you... I have given them the glory that you gave me, that they may be one as we are one: I in them and you in me. May they be brought to complete unity to let the world know that you sent me and have loved them even as you have loved me.
>
> (John 17:20-23)

When we do this and follow the battle plan outlined by Paul, when we follow the model and pattern of Jesus and keep in continual contact and communication with God through prayer, we enter into a state of ceaseless prayer, which the Bible calls "pray(ing) continually" (1 Thessalonians 5:17).

Many Christians claim, "But I'm not very good at prayer."

It's probably the fault of those of us who are professional clergy, that many Christians don't feel as if they are very good at prayer. We professionals have been known to, at times, wax eloquent in prayer. We mix biblical references with subtle nuance, and we use flowery speech and fancy language to express matters of the heart. Sometimes we even shift and revert to preaching in our prayers. No wonder the idea of praying in public is intimidating to the average church-goer. Who would want to sing after Pavarotti; who would want to dance after Michael Jackson?

Here is the good news. You are probably much better at praying than you think you are. This is because, at its essence, prayer is just talking with God. Here is the wonderful truth: if you are good at talking, you will probably be pretty good at praying. Prayer is just talk. If you can talk, you can pray.

It gets even better. Do you tend to worry? If you are a worrier, then you have the potential to be a champion at prayer. After all, worry is just talking with ourselves about our problems, which by the way is rather ineffective (and even neurotic). Prayer, in distinction, is talking to God about our problems, rather than talking with ourselves. We merely have to stop talking inside our heads with ourselves, and bring the conversation to God instead. Prayer is talking with God; it's that simple.

I love the story of an incident involving President Lyndon Johnson, who had sort of a rough, abrupt personality. One day he invited Bill Moyers (who later became a well-known TV journalist) into the private family quarters at the White House. Moyers, at that time, was a special assistant to the President. Johnson knew that Moyers, before he was involved in government, had been a Baptist minister in east Texas, so he asked him to say grace at their family table. Moyers proceeded to bow his head, and then very softly began praying.

Johnson, with his normal bluster and bravado, interrupted Moyer's prayer. He said, "Wait, Bill, I can't hear you. Speak up."

Moyer's response was marvelous. Without raising his head he

said quietly, "Mr. President, I wasn't addressing you."

Prayer is talking to God. Even presidents get second billing.

God's battle plan: It's not difficult, but it is effective

This is God's battle plan, his case-proven strategy for us to live the victorious, abundant Christian life. Our job is to pray. I know many believers are disappointed with this plan; they want something more snappy, some strategy more clever or complex. Christians often like witty plans such as '5 easy steps to spiritual victory,' or 'Seven keys to raise great kids.' But rather than giving us 5 or 7 brainy ideas, Paul simply says, "Your battle plan is to pray."

Which is a brilliant strategy, and it is exactly what we need. When we pray, *God becomes more directly involved*, which makes the crucial difference in our lives. God, as it is often said, is a gentleman. He will not force his love upon us, and he will not demand that we follow his plan. In fact, it is amazing to me how often God allows us to follow our own knuckle-headed plans, knowing all along that we are bound to fail. Like the father of the prodigal son, our heavenly Father gives us more than we deserve, and watches as we take the wrong turn in life, away from him and towards the far country. Yet he lets us go; he doesn't try to prevent or control us. He is the Lord of a voluntary army, not a conscripted or forced militia.

So the revealing question is this: do I live my life on my own power and seldom involve God in the day-to-day issues of my life, or do I sufficiently call on God in prayer? There is a balance here that is important: we want neither to concentrate only on prayer (Jesus not only prayed, but he also lived a life of compassion and action)

225

nor focus only on personal effort. How can we keep these factors in balance?

In my own life, I have developed what people in our church call *Rick's rule for prayer*. It is a simple method by which we can gauge whether we have prayed enough. Here it is: ask God more than others. When we have a need for volunteers in our church, the leaders try to ask God first and fervently. Only then do we go to the congregation and express the need. The same is true if our church has a financial need, facilities need, or a staffing need—essentially, any need.

The same is true at home. When I want my kids to change a behavior, I try to ask God more than I bug them. When I need to accomplish something myself, I ask God more than I pressure myself. I even try to ask God more than I nag my wife. I'm not saying I do this perfectly, and have never bugged my kids or nagged my wife. But believe me, I would be much worse at those things were I not trying to apply *Rick's rule for prayer*.

Try this at work. Do you want your employees, your coworkers, or your employer to change? Try to ask God more about them than you complain to others, and see what happens. What about your neighborhood? Do you have anyone you wish would shape up? Try asking God more than talking with others about this. Do you wish our politicians would do something different? Attempt praying for them more than you complain about them. Do you wish you had more friends? Try *Rick's rule for prayer* and put the matter, first and foremost, in God's hands. He still answers prayer, and the results are better than when we cajole or sweet-talk others into doing what we want.

In fact, let's stop talking about it and pray right now:

Lord,
> I admit it: I'm a complainer and a worrier.
> I tend to bug and nag and pester others
> > in order to get what I want or need.
>
> I'm used to getting things done by the sweat of my brow
> > and by the power of my tongue.
>
> And what I can't get by force or manipulation,
> > I worry about.
>
> I am anxious, I lose sleep, and I fret and frown.
> I spend most of the day talking to myself
> > about my problems and troubles.
>
> I need an extreme makeover.
> I want to be more like Jesus,
> > who talked continually with you
> > and who seemed to talk more with you than others.
>
> Help me learn to ask you more than I ask others,
> > and talk with you more than I worry to myself.
>
> In Jesus' name, Amen.

Our ultimate battle plan is to keep praying

Our super-powerful, offensive weapon against the darkness of evil is the Word of God, as we learned in the last chapter ("Take up the sword of the Spirit, which is the Word of God"). But our ultimate battle plan is outlined by Paul in Ephesians 6:18: "And pray in the Spirit in all occasions with all kinds of prayers and requests."

What kind of army would go into battle without a battle-plan? What kind of soldier would go into battle without a strategy? There is a simple name for an army who would go into a battle without a plan or tactics: *losers*. Likewise, if we go to war against the prince of darkness without a stratagem, we will lose. We will be defeated.

But dear reader, rest in this glorious insight: we don't have to figure out our own battle plan for tomorrow. We don't have to create our own strategies to defeat Satan in the days ahead. It is already right there in the Bible. Let what Paul said sink deeply into your soul, "Pray in the Spirit[72] on all occasions." That is our battle plan for tomorrow. When we get up in the morning, what is the first thing God wants us to do? Pray. When we sit down to breakfast, what is the next thing God wants us to do? Pray. As we get in our cars to drive to work, what are we supposed to do? Pray. Especially on the freeways, pray! (By the way, it is perfectly acceptable to pray with our eyes open on the freeways. The Bible never says we must close our eyes when we pray.)

The same is true for the rest of our day. At work, our battle plan is to pray. If we run into a conflict at work, we pray. If something good happens, we pray. And when we come home to our family, what do we do? Pray. Finally, when we lay our heads down upon our pillows to sleep, we are to pray. As David wrote,

> Let the light of your face shine upon us, O Lord.
> You have filled my heart with greater joy
>   than when their grain and new wine abound.
> I will lie down and sleep in peace,

---

72 There are groups of Christians who interpret this passage, "Pray in the Spirit," as equivalent to "Pray in tongues." Though I believe that is one way to pray in the Spirit, I do not believe it is the only nor even the preferred way. Not only is there no record of Jesus praying in tongues (which surely would have been evidenced and recorded in Jesus' life, if it were intended to be the normative proof of the baptism of the Spirit), but when Paul intends to reference tongues, he does so. Paul is not oblique in his teachings. "Pray in the Spirit" simply means to pray by the power and through the agency of the Holy Spirit, which is also referred to as the Spirit of Christ.

for you alone, O Lord,
make me dwell in safety.

(Psalm 4:6-8)

Or, as the children's prayer puts it:

Now I lay me down to sleep,
    I pray the Lord my soul to keep.
If I should die before I wake,
    I pray the Lord my soul to take.

In my opinion, that is a perfectly good prayer for both kids and adults to pray. In fact, it reminds me of the prayer of Jesus, which, according to Luke, was made up of the last words he uttered before his death: "Father, into your hands I commit my spirit" (Luke 23:46).

What better finale could there be in the life of one who lived in constant communion with God, and who maintained constant communication with God? In addition, what better summary could there be to a life of prayer? Again Jesus provides for us the perfect example and model, in this case, for how we are to die. In death, we cannot trust in our own ability to rescue or save ourselves. We have to trust in God, to rest in him. This final prayer of Jesus is the prayer of *shabot*, of rest.

After death, the Bible promises that believers will be carried to heaven, the place of ultimate rest. In Jesus' parable of the rich man and the beggar named Lazarus, the poor, unfortunate beggar dies and is transported by the angels to heaven, where he is carried to repose at Abraham's side (Luke 16:22). In parabolic form, this teaches what the author of Hebrews wrote in prose:

> Therefore, since the promise of entering his rest still stands, let us be careful that none of you be found to have fallen short of it.
>
> (Hebrews 4:1)

> Now we who have believed enter that rest.
>
> (Hebrews 4:3)

> There remains, then, a Sabbath-rest for the people of God; for anyone who enters God's rest also rests from his own work, just as God did from his. Let us, therefore, make every effort to enter that rest.
>
> (Hebrews 4:9-11)

And like a flourish at the end of a bravado performance, the Bible ends with the realities of life after death, which divides neatly into those who will receive never-ending restlessness, and those who will be given perpetual rest. Concerning the former, the Bible says,

> And the smoke of their torment rises for ever and ever. There is no rest by day or night for those who worship the beast and his image, or for anyone who receives the mark of his name.
>
> (Revelation 14:11)

Fortunately, the opposite is true for believers:

> Then I heard a voice from heaven say, "Write: Blessed are the dead who die in the Lord from now on."
> "Yes," says the Spirit, "they will rest from their labor, for their deeds will follow them."
>
> (Revelation 14:13)

And finally, when all spiritual warfare is brought to a close, when the evil one, the principalities and the powers are permanently defeated, they will be thrown into the lake of fire (Revelation 20:7-10). Then, the glorious opposite will happen to those who have trusted in Jesus as Lord and Savior, whose names are written in the book of life (Revelation 20:12). Those who are saved will be ushered into the heavenly city, in which God will "wipe every tear from their eyes. There will be no more death or mourning or crying or pain, for the old order of things has passed away" (Revelation 21:4). Then, in the final chapter of the Bible, the saved will settle into their heavenly home, where no work is necessary because "the river of the water of life" flows freely, and on each side of the river stands "the tree of life, bearing twelve crops of fruit, yielding its fruit every month" (Revelation 22:1-2). The glorious end—or final beginning!—will happen at last, and the redeemed will enter the ultimate rest of royalty, for "they will reign for ever and ever" (Revelation 22:5).

Let's draw near to the throne of grace, as we look forward to the mansion in Glory our Lord is now preparing for us (John 14:2-3; KJV).

> Lord,
>> It seems to be too good to be true:
>>> heaven, paradise, realms of grace,
>>> and mansions in Glory.
>> To think there will be no grief, mourning or pain,
>>> and we will be filled with joy everlasting.
>> To imagine our spirits will finally find rest,
>>> rest in you and rest from our enemy;
>>> this is the answer to our deepest longings and dreams.
>> The spiritual battle that is waged here on earth
>>> will be won and will cease forever.

And we will live in the house of the Lord, forever.
Maranatha! Hallelujah! Verily, verily, may it be so!
Amen. Come Lord Jesus. The grace of the Lord Jesus
be with God's people. Amen.[73]

---

73   Revelation 22:20-21, which are the last sentences in the Bible.

Appendix One

A Compilation of Daily Prayers To Aid in Praying the Armor of God

Now that you have finished reading *How to Protect Those You Love (By Praying the Armor of God)*, it is my sincere hope you will begin to follow this model for prayer on a daily basis. To help you begin this adventure in prayer, each chapter has supplied examples of how I personally pray the armor of God for those I love. Of course, these examples are not meant to be memorized word-for-word, but instead to provide patterns, which you can follow. Feel free (those who are in Christ are free indeed! John 8:36) to change, mold and adapt these prayers to fit your own context and content. These prayers might also serve as springboards, from which you can jump off in different directions in prayer. Once again, feel free to go in prayer where the Spirit leads.

As you begin this journey, you may find it helpful to use these suggested prayers on a daily basis in order to become accustomed to the flow and topics for each day. Over time, they will become so familiar to you that they will come to mind as you work, drive, garden, or whatever. Even as you do other tasks, you can pray the armor of God, almost like a computer program running unnoticed in the background. For instance, I often pray the armor of God for people as I talk with them. It's actually quite enjoyable and enriching to do this, and the fact that they are unaware, for me, is part of the fun.

However, since the prayers are dispersed throughout the book, they are not easy to locate. In order to make *Praying the Armor of God* as easy to learn as possible, this appendix was created to provide a convenient aid for daily use. It is merely a compilation of the prayers from each chapter, put together in this format for convenience.

And don't forget: pray them *aloud*.

Shalom,

Rick Stedman

Everyday:
Get ready to pray the armor of God for those you love

Scripture:

Finally, be strong in the Lord and in his mighty power. Put on the full armor of God so that you can take your stand against the devil's schemes. For our struggle is not against flesh and blood, but against the rulers, against the authorities, against the powers of this dark world and against the spiritual forces of evil in the heavenly realms. Therefore put on the full armor of God, so that when the day of evil comes, you may be able to stand your ground, and after you have done everything, to stand. Stand firm then...

(Ephesians 6:10-14a)

Prayers:

Lord,
I want to learn to put on your full armor through prayer,
and I want my loved ones to do the same.
Teach me, through your Word,
how to pray on the armor of God
for myself and for those I love.
In Jesus' name, Amen.

235

Lord,

I sincerely desire both myself and my loved ones
could put on the full armor of God through prayer.
But Lord, I have enemies who don't want this to happen.
They want us to remain vulnerable and unprotected.
Now that I realize this,
I pray even more urgently and fervently,
please put your armor on me and my loved ones.
In Jesus' name, Amen.

Lord,

I am not strong enough to fight the evil one.
If I try to fight him with my own strength,
I will fail miserably.
In Jesus' name, Amen.

Lord,

I am not strong enough to fight the evil one.
If I try to fight him with my own strength,
I will fail completely.
And if I try to arm myself against him,
I will also fail miserably.
Give me wisdom for how to put on your armor, Lord.
In Jesus' name, Amen.

Lord,

I am not strong enough to fight the evil one.
If I try to fight him with my own strength,
I will fail completely.
And if I try to arm myself against him,
I will fail miserably.
Instead, I ask you to strengthen me, Lord,
with your mighty power.
I ask you to put on me the very character of Christ,

because it's light that overcomes the darkness.
I ask you to put on me your full armor, O God,
    so I can take my stand against the devil's schemes.
In Jesus' name, Amen.

Lord,

My wife (husband, friend, child…)
    Amy (insert name: _____) is also not strong enough
    to fight the evil one.
If she tries to fight him with her own strength,
    she will fail miserably.
And if she tries to arm herself against him,
    she will fail completely.
Instead, I ask you to strengthen her, Lord,
    with your mighty power.
I ask you to put on her the very character of Christ
    because it's light that overcomes the darkness.
I ask you to put on her your full armor, O God,
    so that she can take her stand
    against the devil's schemes.
In Jesus' name, Amen.

Lord,

Please continue to protect my son (daughter, nephew,
    neighbor, friend…) from evil forces.
Please continue to keep his (her) heart turned towards you.
Please help him not desire or give into
    the many temptations at his high school
    (workplace, etc.),
    but keep him (her) pure and clear and sober-minded.
Give him (her) wisdom beyond his years.
Please help him (her) be a light to these kids (adults)
    who need you

and your love so desperately.
In Jesus' name, Amen.

Sunday:
Strap On the Belt of Truth

Scripture:

"Stand firm, then, with the belt of truth buckled around your waist."

(Ephesians 6:14)

Prayers:

Lord,
I am not strong enough to fight the evil one.
If I try to fight him with my own strength,
   I will fail miserably.
And if I try to arm myself against him,
   I will fail completely.
Instead, I ask you to strengthen me, **Lord,**
   with your mighty power.
I ask you to put on me the very character of Christ,
   because it's light that overcomes the darkness.
I ask you to put on me the full armor of God,
   so I can take my stand against the devil's schemes.
In Jesus' name, Amen.

Lord Jesus, help me!
I am in the middle of a war,
   and the enemy is attacking me from all sides.
I am unable to be a person of truth without you.
I am unable to discover truth without you.

I am unable even to be honest with myself without you.
So I ask you, shine your light upon me now,
    open the eyes of my heart to your truth.
I pray this in the name of Jesus, Amen.

Lord,

    I'm on a battlefield
        facing a long and difficult struggle.
    Help me not be caught unprepared,
        but instead help me be ready
    and fully prepared for battle.
    In Jesus' name, Amen.

Lord,

    I pray for your truth to fill my mind.
    But Lord, I live in a world of untruth where
        lying is the norm.
    I am often confused by so much that is said
        in the media, by politicians,
        and even by Christian leaders that disagree.
    Help me, Lord.
        I want to see reality as you see it;
        I want to know your truths
        and be able to discern right and wrong,
        good and evil as you do.
    In Jesus' name, Amen.

Lord,

    I'm starting to get it;
        the light is dawning in my heart and mind.
    I can see now that our world is so messed up,
        confused, and hurtful.
    Because the god of this world,
        the father of lies and hatred and hurt,

has blinded the minds of those who do not
    yet know your Son, the light of the world.
Lord, I pray for those I love;
    take the blindfolds off their minds.
I pray for those I live by and work with;
    take the blindfolds off their hearts.
I pray for those around the world and especially
    for leaders; take the blindfolds off their eyes.
Help us all to see you, your truth, and bring
    your light and hope to a world in darkness.
In Jesus' name, Amen.

Lord,
    I'm (insert name: _____ is) on a battlefield
    facing a dark and deceitful enemy.
Please put on me (him/her) the belt of truth,
    may I (he/she) see through the lies of this world,
    may I (he/she) grasp the truths of your Word,
    may I (he/she) put off falsehood and speak only truth,
    may I (he/she) be able to discern right from wrong,
        good from evil, light from darkness.
And may Jesus, the Truth and the Light,
    live in and through me (him/her).
In Jesus' name, Amen.

Monday: Make Fast the Breastplate of Righteousness

Scripture:

"Stand firm... with the breastplate of righteousness in place."

(Ephesians 6:14)

Prayers:

Lord,
I am not strong enough to fight the evil one.
If I try to fight him with my own strength,
    I will fail miserably.
And if I try to arm myself against him,
    I will fail completely.
Instead, I ask you to strengthen me, *Lord,*
    with your mighty power.
I ask you to put on me the very character of Christ,
    because it's light that overcomes the darkness.
I ask you to put on me the full armor of God,
    so that I can take my stand against the devil's schemes.
In Jesus' name, Amen.

Lord,

> Our culture is broken and twisted,
>> obviously and firmly under the control of the evil one.
> Marital faithfulness is out and divorce is in,
>> commitment is *passé* and cohabitation is *en vogue*.
> Abortion is considered an inviolable right,
>> while praying in public is considered offensive.
> Dear Lord, lying and deceit are now the norms
>> whereas people of honesty are the exceptions.
> Even our TV shows, during the evening family hour,
>> are full of foul language, vivid violence, and naked sexuality.
> We are lost—lost and bereft of any sense of your righteousness,
>> and we cannot find our way back.
> I beg you to put on us the breastplate of righteousness,
>> so that we can take our stand against the devil's schemes.
> In Jesus' name, Amen.

Lord,

> We are aghast at the moral depravity
>> that surrounds us today.
> We live among people that would not only sell themselves
>> for the right price (becoming prostitutes!),
>> but they would sell out their spouse, their kids,
>> their church and their country.
> Good God, many would even kill for money.
> Please, dear God, we pray that you protect us
>> and our loved ones from this world of wickedness.
> We pray you put on us your breastplate of righteousness.
> In Jesus' name, Amen.

Lord,

> Now I get it: our society is broken
>> because I am broken.
> I am broken and twisted,

and am myself firmly under the control of the evil one.
I do the very things I do not wish to do,
    and I do not do the things I wish to do.
I often speak before thinking,
    and also often fail to speak up when I should.
I criticize others for their unrighteous behavior,
    but seldom confess
    the depths of my own unrighteousness.
My thought life is sometimes filled with notions
    that I would be embarrassed if others knew.
If heaven is a perfect place,
    then I am clearly disqualified,
    even though others consider me to be
    a pretty good person.
I now see clearly
    that being a good person is not good enough.
I need you to forgive me,
    to wash me as white as snow,
    to remember my sins no more,
    to cleanse me of all unrighteousness.
In other words, I need a Savior.
    I ask Jesus Christ to be my Lord and Savior,
    and I commit the rest of my life to him and his service.
I ask you to place on me the breastplate of righteousness,
    so that I can take my stand against the devil's schemes.
In Jesus' name, Amen.

Lord,

I now understand the source of my problems,
    the reason I keep making poor choices and bad decisions:
    my heart is a liar!
My heart is not just deceitful,
    it is deceitful above all things.
It tells me to go right when I should turn left,

to be silent when I should speak up,
to buy or keep when I should give.
Maybe the wisest way for me to live
would be to do the opposite of what my heart suggests,
just as it is usually wise to do the opposite
of what the elites of our secular culture recommend.
What can I do?
I can't trust myself and I can't trust my culture!
Lord, I need you to guide me and reveal to me
what true righteousness means,
and what godly wisdom entails.
Please help me, God,
In Jesus' name, Amen.

Lord,

I'm sorry.
I've lived all these years as a Christian,
but my heart has been unprotected and undervalued.
I haven't worn your breastplate of righteousness.
I've heard things that I should not have heard,
seen things I should have not seen,
and done things I should not have done.
I've let all kinds of junk into my heart,
while failing to store enough of your wisdom and Word there.
Like King David, I need a new heart.
Not just a tune-up or a makeover,
I need a completely fresh start, a new creation.
I ask you to create a clean, pure heart within me.
Help me store good things in my heart,
so the overflow of my heart will be
a blessing to others and an honor to you.
Please put your breastplate of righteousness on me,
for now and evermore.
In the name of the only Righteous One, Jesus, Amen.

Lord,

I'm really worried about these people I love:
(_____insert names here_____),
they have wandered from your path of righteousness,
and their hearts have been left unprotected and at risk.
They aren't wearing your breastplate of righteousness.
They've heard things that they should not have heard,
seen things they should have not seen,
and done things they should not have done.
They've let all kinds of junk into their hearts,
while failing to store enough of your love and Word there.
Like King David, they each need a new heart.
Not just a tune-up or a makeover,
they need completely fresh starts, to be new creations.
I ask you to create a clean, pure heart within them.
Help them store good things in their hearts,
so the overflow of their hearts will be
a blessing to others and an honor to you.
Please put your breastplate of righteousness on them,
for now and evermore.
In the name of the only Righteous One, Jesus, Amen.

Dear

loving heavenly Father,
I pray on this Monday that you
make fast the breastplate of righteousness.
I pray for (insert names of spouse and children),
that you put on them the breastplate of righteousness
and fill their hearts with your Word and love.
I pray for (insert names of extended family members),
that you put on them the breastplate of righteousness
and guide them today on the paths of righteousness
for your name's sake.
I pray for (insert names of church members and leaders),

that you put on them the breastplate of righteousness
and protect them from the evil one,
who desires to divide and destroy.
I pray for (<u>insert names of community and political leaders</u>),
that you put on them the breastplate of righteousness
and help them hear your voice
in a world filled with demonic noise and nonsense.
I pray for (<u>insert names of international leaders dealing
with crises around the world</u>),
that you put on them the breastplate of righteousness
and that if they do not yet know the love of God in Jesus,
that you would lead them
to that all-important discovery.
May the whole earth be filled with your love,
your truth, your joy, and your will,
so that righteousness and peace may kiss together,
and justice may roll down like mighty waters.
I pray this in the name of the King of Righteousness,
Jesus the only one who is Good, Amen.

Tuesday:
Tread in the Shoes of Peace

Scripture:

"…and with your feet fitted with the readiness that comes from the gospel of peace."

(Ephesians 6:15)

Prayers:

Lord,
I am not strong enough to fight the evil one.
If I try to fight him with my own strength,
I will fail miserably.
And if I try to arm myself against him,
I will fail completely.
Instead, I ask you to strengthen me, *Lord,*
with your mighty power.
I ask you to put on me the very character of Christ,
because it's light that overcomes the darkness.
I ask you to put on me the full armor of God,
so that I can take my stand against the devil's schemes.
In Jesus' name. Amen.

Lord,
I'm so concerned about the high failure rate
of relationships in today's culture.
I'm worried that someone I love will fail in their marriage,
that a person I care about will have trouble with their kids,

248

or a church will experience a demon-inspired split.
I'm anxious that some of my kids or grandkids may get divorced
    or—God forbid—it could even happen to me.
God, is there anything I can do?
Is there some way I can help families
    survive the tough times;
    is there something I can do
    to help people deal with the problems
    which inevitably come in every life?
Show me, O *Lord,* according to your word,
    how I can be a model of peace
    to my family and friends now,
    and generationally bless those that will come after me.
In Jesus' name, Amen.

Lord,

I feel like Noah: I live among the unrighteous.
I feel like David: I'm facing a giant with a little slingshot.
I feel like Elijah: I seem to be the only one left serving you.
But Lord,
    I know you put me in this neighborhood for a reason,
    and I know you put my neighbors here for a purpose too.
But we have had some conflicts lately,
    unkind deeds were done,
    harsh words were said,
    feelings were hurt.
Lord, some of my neighbors I don't even want to see,
    others I'd like to give a kick in the pants.
So I need you to make me a peacemaker.
    I can't do it myself.
Let me treat others like Jesus would treat them,
    let me forgive them, though they may treat me poorly,
    even as Christ forgave those who crucified him.
Let me speak words seasoned with grace,

even though they don't deserve them.
Because you, O Lord, do not treat me like I deserve,
    you give me grace that I have not earned,
    and you speak to me with kindness beyond measure.
I want to be like you, O *Lord,* in this neighborhood,
    not like the evil one that others seem to be imitating.
I'd even ask you to do a miracle of reconciliation,
    since I know that is your specialty.
Please fill me now with your peace that passes understanding,
    and let your peace flow through me to others.
In Jesus' name, Amen.

Lord,
    This world is full of conflict, quarrels and even wars;
        though we claim to be people who desire peace,
        we seem to find no end to the ways we
        disagree with one another,
        destroy unity,
        and demolish community.
Husbands and wives begin marriages
        promising undying love to one another,
        yet too often end in divorce court,
        dividing up not only bank accounts
        and household possessions,
        but also siblings and parents.
Neighbors fight over trivial matters,
        politicians fight for power and prestige over principle,
        and nations fight and sacrifice
        the very blood and lives of their young men.
Even Christians find minutiae to argue about,
        dividing into fractured denominations
        and churches split almost like clockwork.
God help us!
We obviously cannot keep the peace on our own,

and the Evil One, the prince of division,
wins the battles all too often.
We need you, O God, to arm us with your peace.
May the Prince of Peace himself fill our lives,
    may his peace rule in our marriages and families,
    may his peace pervade our communities and nations,
    and may his church emphasize his peace and unity
    more than our non-essential differences.
In the name of Jesus we pray, Amen.

Lord,

I pray for my spouse/friend _____
    that you would put on him/her the shoes of peace.
Fill him/her today, Father, Son and Holy Spirit,
    fill him/her with the unity of the Trinity,
    fill him/her with the very love you have shared
    within yourself, O God, from eternity.
When difficult people (especially me!)
    bring conflict into his/her life,
    help him/her to be the peacemaker.
When differences and disagreements arise,
    guide him/her to know what are essentials,
    what are non-essentials,
    and how he/she can always act in love.
In this world where friendships and families seldom last,
    where divorce, betrayals and even wars abound,
    give him/her the jungle boots of peace,
    strong enough to endure
    the battles the Foe will throw at him/her.
And especially help him/her know,
    in the deepest parts of his/her heart and soul,
    that because of Jesus Christ
    he/she is at peace with you, O God,
    now and forevermore.

And that one day he/she and his/her loved ones in Christ,
    will be reunited in Glory and serenity for eternity
In Jesus' name I pray, Amen.

Lord,

The evil one seeks to divide and conquer,
    especially husbands from wives,
    and parents from children.
I pray you would protect the (<u>name</u>) marriage from divorce,
    and the family from fighting and division.
In Jesus' name, Amen.

Lord,

The evil one seeks to divide and conquer,
    including churches and Christian organizations.
So many churches experience divisions and splits
    that it must break your heart, O Lord.
I pray you would protect the (<u>name</u>) church from division,
    that you would give the leaders unity and wisdom,
    and the evil one would not gain a foothold there.
In Jesus' name, Amen.

Lord,

The evil one seeks to divide and conquer,
    including communities, states and even nations.
I pray you would protect our (<u>name</u>) nation from division,
    that you would give the leaders unity and wisdom,
    and the evil one would not gain a foothold there.
Especially help them know how to protect and defend
    the freedoms you have endowed upon all humans,
    but to rarely resort to bloodshed
    to defend those freedoms.
In Jesus' name, Amen.

Wednesday:
Wield the Shield of Faith

Scripture:

"...take up the shield of faith, with which you can extinguish all the flaming arrows of the evil one."

(Ephesians 6:16)

Prayers:

Lord,
> I am not strong enough to fight the evil one.
> If I try to fight him with my own strength,
>> I will fail miserably.
>
> And if I try to arm myself against him,
>> I will fail completely.
>
> Instead, I ask you to strengthen me, ***Lord,***
>> with your mighty power.
>
> I ask you to put on me the very character of Christ,
>> because it's light that overcomes the darkness.
>
> I ask you to put on me the full armor of God,
>> so that I can take my stand against the devil's schemes.
>
> In Jesus' name, Amen.

Lord,
> Misguided people have given faith a bad name,
>> And they have done awful things
>> under the guise of faith.
>
> As a result, faith is taken to be the opposite of truth;

it is seen by many to be an opponent of reason.
Give me your wisdom, *Lord,* so I can be a person of
both faith and facts,
belief and truth,
devotion and evidence.
In Jesus' name, Amen.

Lord,

In this world there are many people
who claim to have faith.
But some of them believe outrageous doctrines,
and even worse, they behave in atrocious ways.
In this world, O *Lord,*
how can I be a person of faith and not foolishness?
The answer, I know, is to be more and more like Jesus.
Since he is named the "Faithful and True" one,
I ask you to fill me with his faith.
In fact, fill me more and more with the Spirit of Christ
so my faith will be his faith,
living in and through me.
In his name I pray, Amen.

Lord,

I will trust in you Lord with all my heart,
and not lean on my own understanding.
In all my ways I will acknowledge you,
and you will make my paths straight.
I will not be wise in my own eyes;
I will fear the Lord and shun evil.
This will bring health to my body
and nourishment to my soul.
In Jesus' name, Amen.

Lord,

Woe to me when I am wise in my own eyes,
and clever in my own sight.
Therefore, as tongues of fire lick up straw
and as dry grass sinks down in the flames,
so my roots will decay
and my flowers blow away like dust;
for I have rejected the law of the Lord Almighty
and spurned the word of the Holy One of Israel.
In Jesus' name, Amen.

Lord,

The fear of the Lord is the beginning of wisdom,
and knowledge of the Holy One is understanding.
In Jesus' name, Amen.

The Lord is my shepherd,
I shall not be in want.
He makes me lie down in green pastures,
he leads me beside still waters,
he restores my soul.
He guides me in paths of righteousness
for his name's sake…

Lord,

My loved ones need protection in this world of evil,
the fiery darts of the evil one
are loaded and aimed towards them.
They need you to be a shield around them.
So I pray you put on them, today and every day,
your shield of faith,
which you have promised will protect them from
all the flaming arrows of the enemy.
Help them also to fully understand

that their shield was never designed to be used alone.
It only works when they are in group formation,
     working together as a spiritual team, a family.
In other words, they need to be church members.
Committed, involved, enduring church members.
Lead them to a Christ-centered, Bible-based, Spirit-filled
     church in which they can be treasured and challenged,
     a church in which they will be accountable.
Protect them, O God, in your will and for your glory.
In Jesus' name, Amen.

Thursday: Think Within the Helmet of Salvation

Scripture:

"Take the helmet of salvation."

(Ephesians 6:17)

Prayers:

Lord,

People today don't take your existence seriously
and they even are flippant and casual
when talking about your enemy, the devil.
They act as if life is a big game, as if existence is like
an appearance on The Price is Right
or a spin on The Wheel of Fortune TV show.
But life is not a game,
and the consequences are eternal.
So I ask you to put your full armor, O God,
on me and on those I love.
We need your protection from the enemy,
especially our minds, thoughts and attitudes.
Put on us your helmet of salvation, O Lord,
so we can think clearly and correctly.
In Jesus' name, Amen.

Lord God,

    I admit I am not perfect and not pure.

    I have messed up tons of times in life,

        and I'm sure I will do so until the day I die.

    Plus, there's nothing I can to fix this or forgive myself.

    I can't completely stop messing up or sinning,

        and I can't purify or become perfect on my own.

    So I ask you, dear Father, to forgive my sins

        by the blood and in the name of your Son Jesus Christ.

    I want to be a Christian,

        I repent of my past sins and prideful life,

        and I confess my wayward ways.

    I want to follow Jesus all the days of my life

        I want to be a part of your Kingdom, now and forever.

    I want in on the party!

    In the name of Jesus,

        the one and only Savior, Amen.

Lord God,

    I will not be anxious about anything,

        but in everything,

        by prayer and petition,

        with thanksgiving,

        I will present my requests to God.

    And the peace of God,

        which transcends understanding,

        will guard my heart and mind in Christ Jesus.

    Whatever is true,

        whatever is noble,

        whatever is right,

        whatever is lovely,

        whatever is admirable,

        if anything is excellent,

        or praiseworthy,

I will think on these things.
In Jesus' name, Amen.

Lord God,

I am blessed

for I walk not in the counsel of the wicked,

or stand in the way of sinners

or sit in the seat of mockers.

But my delight is in the law of the Lord,

and on his law I meditate day and night.

I am like a tree planted by streams of water,

which yields its fruit in season

and whose leaf does not wither.

Whatever I do prospers.

In Jesus' name, Amen.

Lord God,

Do not let any unwholesome talk come out of my mouth,

but only what is helpful

for building others up according to their needs,

that it may benefit those who listen.

And do not let me grieve the Holy Spirit of God,

with whom I was sealed for the day of redemption.

Help me get rid of all bitterness,

rage and anger, brawling and slander,

along with every form of malice.

Help me be kind and compassionate to others,

forgiving each other,

just as, in Christ, God forgave me

In Jesus' name, Amen.

The LORD

is my shepherd,

I shall not be in want.

He makes me lie down in green pastures,
    he leads me beside quiet waters,
    he restores my soul;
    he guides me in the paths of righteousness
    for his name's sake.
Even though I walk through
    the valley of the shadow of death,
    I fear no evil, for you are with me;
    your rod and your staff, they comfort me.
You prepare a table before me
    in the presence of my enemies;
    you have anointed my head with oil;
    my cup overflows.
Surely goodness and love
    will follow me all the days of my life,
    and I will dwell in the house of the Lord forever.
In Jesus' name, Amen.

Lord,

Thank you that, by your grace, I saw the light,
    I realized I was a sinner and an imperfect person,
    and I also grasped that heaven is a perfect place.
There's just no way I can save or forgive myself,
    and there's no way heaven will remain perfect if you
    let in 'pretty good' people like me.
I need to be purified, forgiven, and made perfect,
    and I know only Jesus can do that for me.
So I've asked Jesus Christ to be my Lord and Savior,
    and I know my assurance of being saved is
    firmly protected and kept by his power, not mine.
Thank you for the promise of salvation,
    that you have written my name
    in the Lamb's book of life,
    and that you are now preparing for me

a mansion in Glory.
In Jesus' name, Amen.

Lord,

My mind is filled with
    worries, fears, and impure thoughts.
My mind is a mess.
Will you please come in and take control,
    clean up the contents of my mind?
I ask you to put on me the helmet of salvation
    and teach me to think within that worldview.
Help me take captive every thought
    to make it obedient to Christ.
I ask you help me not be conformed to this world,
    but please, dear Lord,
    transform me by the renewing of my mind.
Then I will be able to test and approve what your will is,
    and I will not think more highly of myself than I ought.
In Jesus' name, Amen.

Lord,

    I want to learn to meditate upon your Word,
        I want to be filled with your thoughts,
        I want to be saturated in your ways,
        I want to be overflowing with your love.
    I ask you to put your helmet of salvation upon me today
        and fill me with the very mind of Christ.
    I don't want to be a positive-thinker,
        or a possibility-thinker,
        or a human-potential-thinker.
    I want to be a Jesus-thinker,
        I want to think about Jesus all the time.
    I want to be a Scripture-thinker,
        I want to be meditating upon your Word constantly.

I want you, O God,
    to think your thoughts inside me!
In Jesus' name, Amen.

Friday:
Fight with the Sword of the Spirit

Scripture:

"Take…the sword of the Spirit, which is the Word of God."
(Ephesians 6:17)

Prayers:

Lord,
We come to you on Fridays,
   so very thankful for your mercy, grace and love.
We are overwhelmed with how good you are to us,
   and overjoyed everyday to walk personally with you.
People around us look forward to the weekend
   to party with drugs and alcohol,
   to anesthetize themselves for a short while,
   to create a temporary, mock version of happiness.
But we want to be filled with your Spirit because
   we know you are the true and unending source
   of lasting joy, peace, and contentment.
Plus, we know you are preparing a feast for us in heaven,
   a celebration that will go on forever,
   a party that will far surpass all earthly parties.
We ask that you put on us and our loved ones, today,
   your very own armor, O God,
   so we can be protected from the evil one,
   whose goal is to keep us out of your eternal party.
We are not powerful enough to defend ourselves from him,

nor wise enough to even recognize all of his schemes.
Protect us this day, we pray,
In the name of Jesus, Amen.

Lord,
> It is written:
>> 'Man does not live by bread alone,
>> but on every word that comes
>> from the mouth of God.'
> It is also written:
>> 'Do not put the Lord your God to the test'.
> So I declare:
>> Away from me, Satan!
> For it is written:
>> Worship the Lord your God, and serve him only.
> In Jesus' name, Amen

Lord,
> Sometimes I feel like crying out in a loud voice,
>> *"Eloi, Eloi, lama sabachthani?"*
>> "My God, my God, why have you forsaken me?"
> O Lord, please hear my prayer,
>> my cry of pain,
>> which you alone fully understand.
> In Jesus' name, Amen.

Lord,
> Thank you that
>> the Word became flesh,
>> and dwelt among us.
> Thank you that
>> we have seen his glory,
>> the glory of the One and Only,
>> who came from the Father,

full of grace and truth.
In Jesus' name, Amen

Lord,

We have been born again,
not of perishable seed,
but of imperishable,
through the living and enduring word of God.
For,
all people are like grass,
and all our glory is like the flowers of the field;
the grass withers and the flowers fail,
but the word of the Lord stands forever.
In Jesus' name, Amen.

O Lord,

How many are my foes!
How many rise up against me!
Many are saying of me,
"God will not deliver him."

Selah

But you are a shield around me, O Lord;
you bestow glory on me and lift up my head.
To the Lord I cry aloud,
and he answers me from his holy hill.

Selah

I will lie down and sleep;
I wake again, because the Lord sustains me.
I will not fear the tens of thousands
drawn up against me on every side.
In the name of Jesus, Amen.

Lord,

My kids today will step into the battle zone;
> they will have the flaming arrows of the enemy
> launched at them all day long.

The enemy is relentless, and his only desire
> for them is to kill and destroy.

Selah

I pray that you would put on them your full armor, O God,
> so they can take their stand against the evil one.

Today I especially pray you help them
> take up the sword of the Spirit,
> which is the Word of God.

Help them become strong in your mighty Word.

Selah

I pray you would plant your Word in their hearts,
> like a mustard seed that will grow large and healthy.

I pray they come to firmly believe
> your Word is trustworthy, logical, and factual.

Help them believe from the top of their heads
> to the tips of their toes,
> that trusting and obeying your Word
> is the smartest thing they will ever do.

I pray your word becomes, in their minds and hearts,
> their daily source for wisdom and guidance.

Selah

In the name of Jesus, Amen.

Saturday:
Steadfastly Pray in the Spirit

Scripture:

"And pray in the Spirit on all occasions with all kinds of prayers and requests. With this in mind, be alert and always keep on praying for all the saints."

(Ephesians 6:18)

Prayers:

Lord,

What a privilege it is to come to you in prayer.
What an honor it is to speak with you personally,
    even the ability to do so is an unfathomable wonder.
I come to you because I am in a battle zone,
    as are those I love.
The evil one is hurling his flaming arrows at us,
    and we need your protection.
Please put on us your very own armor, O God,
    clothe us with Christ!
Teach us today how to draw close to you in prayer,
In Jesus' name, Amen.

Lord,

What a great God you are, Lord Almighty,
    How good you are to us, your followers and children.
No idols ever were said to command people to rest,
    not those of the Canaanites, Egyptians, or Philistines.

You alone truly desire our best interests,
  and command us in ways that are healthy for us.
What a loving heavenly Father you are.
In Jesus' name, Amen.

Lord,

Help me pray in the Spirit on all occasions,
  with all kinds of prayers and requests.
With this in mind, help me be alert
  and always keep on praying for all the saints.
I Pray, dear **Lord,** that whenever I open my mouth,
  words may be given me
so that I will fearlessly make known
  the mystery of the gospel,
    for which I am an ambassador in chains.
I pray that I may declare it fearlessly, as I should.
In Jesus' name, Amen.

Lord,

In you I trust, O my God.
Do not let me be put to shame,
  nor let my enemies triumph over me.
Many are the woes of the wicked,
  but the Lord's unfailing love
  surrounds me because I trust in him.
Some trust in chariots and horses,
  but I trust in the name of the Lord my God.
When I am afraid,
  I will trust in you
In God, whose word I praise,
  in God I trust;
  I will not be afraid.
In Jesus' name, Amen.

Lord,

When _____ is afraid,
    let him/her trust in you
In God, whose word he/she praises,
    in God he/she trusts;
        _____ will not be afraid.
In Jesus' name, Amen

Lord,

Since I have such a great High Priest,
    even Jesus the Son of God,
    let me hold firmly to the faith I profess.
For I do not have a high priest
    who is unable to sympathize
    with my weaknesses,
    but I have one
    who has been tempted in every way,
    just as I am—yet was without sin.
Let me then approach the throne of grace
    with confidence,
    so that I may receive mercy and find grace
    to help in my time of need.
In Jesus' name, Amen.

Lord,

I admit it: I'm a complainer and a worrier.
I tend to bug and nag and pester others
    in order to get what I want or need.
I'm used to getting things done by the sweat of my brow
    and by the power of my tongue.
And what I can't get by force or manipulation,
    I worry about.
I am anxious, I loose sleep, and I fret and frown.
I spend most of the day talking to myself

269

about my problems and troubles.
I need an extreme makeover.
I want to be more like Jesus,
> who talked continually with you
> and who seemed to talk more with you than others.
Help me learn to ask you more than I ask others,
> and talk with you more than I worry to myself.
In Jesus' name, Amen.

Lord,

Let the light of your face shine upon us, O Lord.
You have filled my heat with greater joy
> than when their grain and new wine abound.
I will lie down and sleep in peace,
> for you alone, O *Lord,*
> make me dwell in safety.
In Jesus' name, Amen.

Lord,

Now I lay me down to sleep,
> I pray the Lord my soul to keep.
If I should die before I wake,
> I pray the Lord my soul to take.
In Jesus' name, Amen.

Lord,

Since the promise of entering his rest still stands,
> let us be careful that none of us
> are found to have fallen short of it.
And thank you, Lord,
> that we who have believed enter that rest.
And since there remains, then,
> a Sabbath-rest for the people of God;
> for anyone who enters God's rest

also rests from his own work,
 just as God did from his.
Let us, therefore,
 make every effort to enter that rest.
For a voice from heaven will say,
  "Write: Blessed are the dead
  who die in the Lord from now on."
"Yes," says the Spirit,
  "they will rest from their labor,
  for their deeds will follow them."
In Jesus' name, Amen.

Lord,

It seems too good to be true:
  heaven, paradise, realms of grace,
  and mansions in Glory.
To think there will be no grief, mourning or pain,
  and we will be filled with joy everlasting.
To imagine our spirits will finally find rest,
  rest in you and rest from our enemy,
  this is the answer to our deepest longings and dreams.
The spiritual battle that is waged here on earth
  will be won and will cease forever.
And we will live in the house of the Lord, forever.
  Maranatha!
  Hallelujah!
  Verily, verily, may it be so!
Amen. Come Lord Jesus.
  The grace of the Lord Jesus be with God's people.
Amen.

Appendix Two

Study Questions For Small Group Use

I recommend that this book, *How to Protect Those You Love (By Praying the Armor of God)*, be used in a small group format as a way to learn how to pray. We Christians often talk about prayer, but actually we tend to pray less than we talk about it. A small group setting is a terrific place in which believers can remedy this and learn to pray. Prayer, after all, involves language, and the learning and use of language is a social event.

I recommend a length of nine weeks for this small group study. Or set aside eight if your group desires to skip the first introductory week. Leaders can ask members to acquire the books in advance and read Chapter One before the first meeting. Each group member is to read a chapter before each meeting, and come ready to discuss concepts and ask questions. I suggest that each prayer offered in the course of each chapter be prayed, aloud, by a different member of the group (especially make sure the group leader is not the only one who reads the prayers). Have that person read the prayer aloud first, praying it for himself or herself in the first person. Next, ask the same individual to pray the prayer again, this time for someone he/she loves or for whom he feels a need to pray. Replace the "I," with the person's name, and the "me" and "my" personal pronouns with the appropriate corresponding word. For instance, in the following prayer,

> Lord,
> > I am not strong enough to fight the evil one.
> > If I try to fight him with my own strength,
> > > I will fail miserably...

a person might adjust it accordingly,

> Lord,
> > My cousin Andrew is not strong enough to fight the evil one.
> > If Andrew tries to fight him with his own strength,
> > > he will fail miserably...

In this way, people will experience personally how to pray the armor of God for those they love, and they also will learn how to modify and adjust the prayers from hearing others do so.

Also, this is a terrific study for new Christians, and even non-believers (remember, the vast majority of people pray regardless of whether they are followers of Jesus or not, and even the majority of atheists pray regularly). Almost everyone has a desire to protect loved ones, so don't forget to have every group member pray and invite a friend to join this study.

Week One

Everyday: Get ready to pray the armor of God for those you love

Scripture:

> Finally, be strong in the Lord and in his mighty power.
> Put on the full armor of God so that you can take your
> stand against the devil's schemes. For our struggle is not
> against flesh and blood, but against the rulers, against
> the authorities, against the powers of this dark world and
> against the spiritual forces of evil in the heavenly realms.
> Therefore put on the full armor of God, so that when the
> day of evil comes, you may be able to stand your ground,
> and after you have done everything, to stand. Stand firm
> then...
>
> (Ephesians 6:10-14a)

Group Instructions & Study Questions:

1. Show and Tell: ask each person to take out his or her keys, and
    explain what each key protects. Give a silly award to the person
    with the most keys, such as a fake "Key to the Group" (like the
    "Key to a City" Mayors often give visiting dignitaries) or a unique
    keychain.

    The leaders can, each week, provide the gift or gag gift
    themselves, or they can assign a group member to bring the next

week's gift, along the lines of a 'white elephant' gift. The member doesn't have to spend any money, but just wrap up something funny in their home they don't mind giving away.

2. Open with a prayer that God would help each member of the group learn how to better protect those they love, through the keys given in Ephesians 6.

3. Read aloud and in unison Ephesians 6:10-14a (above).

4. Hand out a copy of *How to Protect Those You Love (By Praying the Armor of God)* to each group member, have them write their names on the inside front cover, and have them agree to read one chapter a week in preparation for the small group meeting. (It's even better if they were able to acquire the book and read Chapter One before the first meeting.)

5. Turn to page 23 and read Ephesians 6:13-18 aloud and in unison. Ask: What are your first impressions when you hear this passage? Does the idea of armor appeal to you or repel you? Why?

6. Ask: Even if the concept of war or fighting is repellent to you, could it be true that there is a spiritual battle being waged about us? What are some evidences that this might be the case? Have different group members read the stories on pages 11-13 and pages 20-21.

7. Ask: How did your parents protect you when you were growing up? Were they overprotective or too lax? Who are you responsible to protect at this point in your life? How do you do that? Do you think parents (or friends) can improve at protecting their family (friends) spiritually?

8. Rick claims that most of us are "failing miserably" at spiritual warfare. Discuss whether you agree or disagree with that claim, and the reason he gives for it (which is found on pages 24-25).

9. Discuss whether Christians can put the armor on themselves, or whether it is better to ask God to put his armor on us (see pages 25-26).

10. Discuss how the concepts of light and darkness relate to spiritual warfare (see page 28). Have you known anyone who focused too much on the darkness? What happened?

11. Hand out the *How to Protect Those You Love (By Praying the Armor of God)* bookmarks (available at adventurechurch.org or rickstedman.com). Talk about how the first letters of the days of the week correspond to a portion of the armor of God. Ask: what other memory devices do you use to remember important details (such as notes on the mirror, or tying a string on a finger as Uncle Billy did in *It's a Wonderful Life*).

    Suggestion: the group may choose to purchase additional bookmarks to distribute as gifts to family members and friends.

12. Turn to Appendix One, "Everyday" (page 235). Ask each person to consecutively read a prayer aloud. One person at a time, go around the circle and ask each person to try to pray a prayer, substituting the name and re-phrasing the pronouns as necessary. Assure people that no one will be forced to pray aloud, but they will be encouraged to give it a try each week.

13. **Homework** for next week: ask each member to bring to the group meeting several belts they own, especially those that are different or unique. Inform them they will vote for most unique belt, ugliest belt, and the belt most likely similar to the type a Roman soldier would wear.

Also, stress the importance of reading Chapters 1 & 2 this week.

Week Two

Sunday: Strap On the Belt of Truth

Scripture:

"Stand firm, then, with the belt of truth buckled around your waist."

(Ephesians 6:14a)

Group Instructions & Study Questions:

1. Show and Tell: ask each group member to show and explain what belts they brought with them, and why they consider them to be unique. Vote for the most unique belt, the ugliest belt, and the belt most likely similar to the type a Roman soldier would wear. Give gag gifts as prizes.

2. Open with a prayer that God would help each member of the group learn how to better protect those they love, through the keys given in Ephesians 6.

3. Read Ephesians 6:14a aloud and in unison (see above).

4. Have each person turn to Chapter Two of *How to Protect Those*

You Love (By Praying the Armor of God). Begin by praying aloud and in unison the prayer on page 33.

5. Dress one group member up in a 'tunic,' by taking an old sheet, tearing it into the appropriate length and width, and cutting a slit for the head. Take a piece of rope and tie it about the person's waist, discussing how this is what the Bible referred to as "girding ones loins."

6. Ask if there are any group members who sew and make their own clothing, or had a parent or grandparent that did so. Discuss how tailored, off-the-shelf clothing is a modern invention, and how our clothing would be different if we lived in the time of Jesus.

7. Ask: Is dishonesty really the norm, as Rick claims on page 43? Discuss the statistics given in the book *The Day America Told the Truth* (page 43-44) and in *Dare to Be True* (page 45). Do these surprise you? Why or why not? If so, which of these statistics is most shocking to you? Why?

8. Ask: Does it surprise you that so many Bible characters lied (see pages 45-46)? Why or why not? If the Bible were really a bunch of made-up stories and legends, would the heroes really be presented as so non-heroic?

9. Read together 2 Corinthians 4:4-6 (found on page 47). Discuss whether the group members have experienced this phenomenon:

that unbelievers seem blind to the truths about God and Jesus, and seem unable to even grasp some of the concepts.

10. Ask: What do you think of Churchill's honesty? Do politicians today talk with this type of candor? Why or why not?

11. Ask: What are some examples of little 'white lies' we sometimes tell each other, in order to not hurt the feelings of those you love? Examples may include: "What a nice outfit you are wearing," "It's nice to see you, too," or "No, that dress does not make you look fat."

12. How about you? Does speaking the truth come easy for you, even when you know it will upset the listener(s)? Or do you have a hard time in this area, and find yourself saying little 'fibs' or falsehoods?

13. Have different group members read a verse each from Matthew 23:13, 15, 16, 17, 18-19, 23-24, 25-26, 27, and 33. What do these verses suggest about Jesus' ability to speak the truth?

14. Turn to Appendix One, "Sunday" (page 239). Ask each person to consecutively read a prayer aloud. One member at a time, go around the circle and ask each person to try to pray a prayer, substituting the name and rephrasing the pronouns as necessary. Assure people once again that no one will be forced to pray aloud, but they will be encouraged to give it a try each week.

15. **Homework** for next week: Ask each member to wear a vest to the group meeting. Let them know there will be a prize for the ugliest vest, the best vest, and the most creative vest. Encourage members to make their own. Tell the story about Rick's son Jesse, who for a "Crazy Christmas Sweater Contest" at his youth group when he was in high school, took a sweater vest and attached a wreath to the front with five candles. He actually lit the candles, and, for a time, was a walking Advent Wreath! Ask them to be creative, but also safe.

Also, ask members to bring to next week's meeting a couple of old magazines they don't mind throwing away, and stress the need or each person to read Chapter Three before the next meeting.

16. Decide who will bring the next week's gifts. Close in prayer.

Week Three

Monday: Make Fast the Breastplate of Righteousness

Scripture:

> "Stand firm… with the breastplate of righteousness in place."
>
> (Ephesians 6:14b)

Group Instructions & Study Questions:

1. Show and Tell: Ask each group member to model the vest they made and/or chose to wear, and to explain why they chose to wear it. Vote for the most unique, the ugliest, and the vest most likely similar to the type a Roman soldier would wear. Give very small gag gifts (such as cookies or candies) as prizes.

2. Open with a prayer that God would help each member of the group learn how to better protect those they love, through the keys given in Ephesians 6.

3. Read Ephesians 6:14b aloud and in unison (see above).

4. Have each person turn to Chapter Three of *How to Protect Those*

You Love (By Praying the Armor of God). Begin by praying aloud and in unison the prayer on page 59.

5. Have several old magazines available (use your own and the ones brought by group members) and ask each person tear or cut out a few examples of unrighteousness, as well as a few examples of righteousness. On a poster board, ask the artistic members (they will love doing this) glue into a collage the examples with the righteous examples of the right and the unrighteousness on the left.

   (No offense intended to left-handed people; 'righteousness' happens to contain the word 'right.' As a humorous aside, though, you might note that in Hebrew, 'left-handed' is literally 'wrong-handed.")

6. Ask: Why did you consider some cuttings to represent righteousness, and what make others unrighteous? How would you define righteousness? Unrighteousness?

7. Do you believe your perceptions and definitions are mere opinions, or do you believe righteousness and unrighteousness can be objectively distinguished? Or, to put it more simply, do the terms 'right' and 'wrong' refer to real, actual qualities, as do 'blue,' 'hot' and even 'funny' and 'sad'?

8. Ask: Do you agree that we live in a world devoid of righteousness (see pages 60-62 and pages 64-65))? Why or why not?

9. Ask: Have you ever known someone who assumed he or she would go to heaven after death, simply by being 'a pretty good person'? Why do you think they made that assumption, especially about such an important matter—where he or she would live for all eternity?

10. Open a package of candy hearts, and have group members choose a heart with the message written on it they prefer. Ask each member to explain why he or she chose that particular heart. (If these are unavailable, make paper hearts and ask each person to write a message.)

11. Ask: Mention an event or decision, in your life, in which you followed your heart and did something that seemed wise at the time, but later you realized was a very poor and foolish choice?

    Examples might include: A purchase? An investment? A romantic involvement? A decision involving one's family, friends, or church? How do you think it was possible for your hearts to lead you so astray?

12. Ask: Why do you think the Bible describes the righteousness as a "heart issue," as Rick mentioned on pages 72-74? What is it about the heart that makes it the place humans choose between right and wrong?

13. Have different group members read a verse each from Psalm 119:11, Proverbs 3:1-4, Proverbs 3:5-6, Ephesians 5:19-20, and

Luke 6:43-45. What do these verses suggest about how we are to manage our hearts?

14. Turn to Appendix One, "Monday" (page 242). Ask each person to consecutively read a prayer aloud. One member at a time, go around the circle and ask each person to try to pray a prayer, substituting the name and rephrasing the pronouns as necessary.

15. **Homework** for next week: ask each member to wear their craziest shoes to the group meeting. Let them know there will be a prize for the most original shoes. Encourage members to try and be inventive and outlandish, and remind them to read Chapter 4 before the meeting.

16. Decide who will bring the next week's gifts. Close in prayer.

Week Four

Tuesday: Tread in the Shoes of Peace

Scripture:

"...and with your feet fitted with the readiness that comes from the gospel of peace."

(Ephesians 6:15)

Group Instructions & Study Questions:

1. Show and Tell: It's time for the 'Crazy Shoe Contest.' Ask each group member to model the shoes they wore, and to explain why they believe them to be original. Vote for the most creative pair of shoes, and discuss which shoes are most similar to the type a Roman soldier would wear. Give a small gag gift as a prize.

2. Open with a prayer that God would help each member of the group learn how to better protect those they love, through the keys given in Ephesians 6.

3. Read Ephesians 6:15 aloud and in unison (see above).

4. Have each person turn to Chapter Four of *How to Protect Those*

You Love (By Praying the Armor of God). Begin by praying aloud and in unison the prayer on page 88.

5. Ask: Describe a close friendship you once had that fell apart. What were the factors that led to the failure of the friendship? In hindsight, is there anything you would do differently to try to avoid what happened?

6. Discuss the fact that the word 'demon' literally means 'divider,' and that Satan himself might therefore be called the Great Divider. What are some areas in which demons are divisive, and what are some ways in which that divisiveness is manifested?

7. Have you ever had a job or played in a sport that required a special type of shoe? What was it? Were the shoes of use anywhere else? Did the shoes require any special preparation? Discuss how this related to our need to 'prepare' for conflict in advance by being clothed with and attitude of peace.

8. Have different group members read a verse each from John 14:27, John 16:33, Philippians 4:6-7, Romans 13:14, Galatians 2:20 and Colossians 3:15. How do these verses suggest we can become persons of peace?

9. Ask: Is it always possible to keep the peace? Read and discuss Romans 12:18.

10. Ask: Is pacifism always right and violence always wrong? Read and discuss Isaiah 53:4-9 and John 2:13-16. How do these Scriptures relate to the need for us to be peacemakers in our world today?

11. Are any group members wearing crosses? Do any display crosses on the walls of their homes? (If the host family has a cross, maybe they could fetch it now and share why they choose to display it.)

    The cross is a ubiquitous symbol today. It is worn by many as jewelry, and is commonly displayed in artwork or sculpture in homes, both Christian and non-Christian. For instance, it's Ozzy Ozborne's symbol of choice, even though he was the lead singer for the notorious band *Black Sabbath*. Yet crosses are also removed from public property as offensive to atheists. What is it about the cross that makes it offensive to some, precious to others, and benign to the rest?

12. Read Genesis 13:8 and discuss the decision Abraham made. Ask: Do you think you would have made the same choice? Why or why not?

13. Turn to Appendix One, "Tuesday" (page 248). Ask each person to consecutively read a prayer aloud. One member at a time, go around the circle and ask each person to try to pray a prayer, substituting the name and rephrasing the pronouns as necessary.

14. **Homework** for next week: It's 'Shield Day,' so ask each member

to bring something that works as a 'shield,' in some fashion, in today's world. Let them know there will be a prize for the 'shield' that most corresponds to the spiritual message Paul was trying to convey by the Roman shield. Encourage members to try and think deeply about this one. For instance: sunglasses shield our eyes from harmful light, an umbrella shields us from the rain, etc.

15. Decide who will bring the next week's gifts. Close in prayer.

Week Five

Wednesday: Wield the Shield of Faith

Scripture:

> "...take up the shield of faith, with which you can extinguish all the flaming arrows of the evil one."
>
> (Ephesians 6:16)

Group Instructions & Study Questions:

1. Show and Tell: It's time for the 'In the Spirit of the Shield' contest. Ask each group member to explain the 'shields' they brought, and how they correspond with the spiritual shield of Ephesians 6:16. Vote for the best shield, and give a small gag gift as a prize.

2. Open with a prayer that God would help each member of the group learn how to better protect those they love, through the keys given in Ephesians 6.

3. Read Ephesians 6:16 aloud and in unison (see above).

4. Have each person turn to Chapter Five of *How to Protect Those You Love (By Praying the Armor of God)*. Begin by praying aloud

and in unison the prayer on page 114.

5. Ask: What is your favorite day of the week? Least favorite? Why do you think Wednesdays have been so disliked over the centuries?

6. Ask: Some people talk as if faith is opposed to reason. Did you ever feel this way, that people of faith were ignorant or at least not using their brains very well? Why? Were there specific influences that led you to that opinion? How do you feel about it now?

7. Rick claims on page 121 that "...there would be no science, no medicine, no philosophy, no commerce, no communities or cultures, and certainly no marriage or families, if it were not for faith." Why do you think this is true or untrue?

8. Have different group members read a verse each from Hebrews 11:1; Genesis 15:6; Romans 4:3, 9; Habakkuk 2:4; and Romans 1:17. Can your group summarize, in contemporary words, the main point of these passages?

9. We discussed in Chapter Three how people today are taught to follow their own hearts, yet in this chapter we are reminded that they also are warned against having faith. Do you think this is a contradiction? Is it possible to follow one's heart and intuitions and not have faith in oneself?

10. Have different group members read a verse each from Proverbs

1:7; 3:5-8; 26:12; Isaiah 5:21, 24; Psalm 23:1-3. The Bible makes it clear that we are to live by faith in God, which means trusting God and following his ways, rather than by faith in ourselves. Do you struggle with this? Why or why not?

11. Rick noted the shield specified by Paul in Ephesians 6:16 is the larger Roman shield, rather than the smaller shield which was used in hand to hand combat. Why did Paul choose one rather than the other?

12. Rick says on page 131, "Here's the point: the shield of faith was never meant to be used by solo Christians. The shield of faith is to be used in formation, alongside other Christians who have also taken up their shield, their *thureos*, of faith." Based on this, how do you believe God designed Christians to function: alone or with others, and to what extent? Why?

13. Read aloud Romans 12:1-8 and 1 Corinthians 12:12-26. Discuss: if the Bible says we are like members of the body, how deeply involved does that imply Christians should be in their churches?

14. Rick believes that membership in the church, the Body of Christ, should not be just global, but also local. Are you a member of your local church? Why or why not?

15. Turn to Appendix One, "Wednesday" (page 253). Ask each person to consecutively read a prayer aloud. One member at a time, go

around the circle and ask each person to try to pray a prayer, substituting the name and rephrasing the pronouns as necessary.

16. **Homework** for next week: it's the perennial favorite, 'Crazy Hat Contest,' so ask each member to bring their favorite hat, helmet, etc, along with whatever hats they think might win the awards for ugliest, most creative, or best spiritually representative hat.

17. Decide who will bring the next week's gifts. Close in prayer.

Week Six

Thursday: Think Within the Helmet of Salvation

Scripture:

"Take the helmet of salvation."

(Ephesians 6:17)

Group Instructions & Study Questions:

1. Show and Tell: It's time for the contest, which is a perennial favorite, The 'Crazy Hat' contest. Ask each group member to model the hats they brought, and vote one again for the ugliest, the most creative, and the most spiritually representative hat. Give small gag gifts as prizes.

2. Before beginning the lesson, discuss whether the group intends to continue meeting after this study concludes after two more sessions. If so, begin discussion of what book of the Bible the members are interested in studying, or what topic of study. Samples of various home Bible studies are available at Christian bookstores, online, and often can be borrowed from a pastor or other small group leader.

   This is an area in which it is very beneficial for small group leaders to meet regularly with other leaders: they can swap resources and share success stories. If your church does not do this regularly, then find the names of a few other small group leaders in your fellowship and set up an informal meeting. Spend some time sharing topics, resources, successes and challenges. Then end the meeting in prayer. You'll be glad you did—and so will others.

3. Open with a prayer that God would help each member of the group learn how to better protect those they love, through the keys given in Ephesians 6.

4. Read Ephesians 6:17 aloud and in unison (see above).

5. Have each person turn to Chapter Six of *How to Protect Those You Love (By Praying the Armor of God)*. Begin by praying aloud and in unison the prayer on page 142.

6. Ask: what are some advertising jingles that people remember from TV commercials, such as Wendy's "Where's the beef," Alka-Seltzer's "I can't believe I ate the whole thing," to Super Bowl champions saying, "I'm going to Disneyland." Nominate and then vote for the group's choice of the all-time best commercial jingle.

7. Ask: do you agree that there is a battle going on today for the minds of people? Do you think this is a battle going on in the natural or in the spiritual realm? Why?

8. Rick claims that one of the battles is over theories of who will go to heaven. Read 1 John 1:5, 7, 9; Revelation 21:27, and discuss what that implies about a "pretty good person" getting into heaven.

9. Ask: Do group members know anyone who assumes they will go to heaven because he/she is a "pretty good person"? Describe that person, and discuss how Christians should approach these relationships.

10. Read Philippians 4:6-7. Discuss: Are there any group members who are worry-warts? Have each person describe one issue in life that he/she tends to worry about.

11. Read 2 Corinthians 10:3-5. Ask: How can Christians take captive every thought for Christ? How can we win the war on the battlefield in our brain?

12. Ask: when you hear the word "meditation," what is the first image that comes to your mind? How is Christian meditation different from Eastern (such as Hindu or Buddhist) meditation?

13. Have each group member pick a favorite Scripture to memorize this week and upon which they will try to meditate. Have them write down their thoughts and insights, based on the week-long experiment, to share with the group next week.

14. Turn to Appendix One, "Thursday" (page 257). Ask each person

to consecutively read a prayer aloud. One member at a time, go around the circle and ask each person to try to pray a prayer, substituting the name and rephrasing the pronouns as necessary.

15. **Homework** for next week: It's too risky to have a "weapons" show and tell, so instead ask each member to bring their favorite Bibles. Possible prizes can be awarded for the oldest, the biggest, and the most worn-by-use.

16. Decide who will bring the next week's gifts. Close in prayer.

Week Seven

Friday: Fight with the Sword of the Spirit

Scripture:

"Take...the sword of the Spirit, which is the Word of God."

(Ephesians 6:17)

Group Instructions & Study Questions:

1. Show and Tell: It's time for "Bible Show and Tell." Ask each member to display their Bibles and tell any relevant stories, such as how long a certain Bible has been in his/her family, etc. Possible prizes can be awarded for the oldest, the biggest, and the most worn-by-use. Give small gifts as prizes.

    Ask each group member to explain which Bible is their personal favorite and why. Discuss how a specific Bible can become a person's favorite, much like a particular sword often became the weapon of choice for a soldier. Discuss any parallels between the two.

2. Before beginning the lesson, discuss again whether the group

298

intends to continue meeting. If so, begin to narrow down the options for which study the group wants to pursue. Share samples of study materials, gathered by both the leader and group members.

3. Open with a prayer that God would help each member of the group learn how to better protect those they love, through the keys given in Ephesians 6.

4. Read Ephesians 6:17 aloud and in unison (see above).

5. Have each person turn to Chapter Seven of *How to Protect Those You Love (By Praying the Armor of God)*. Begin by praying aloud and in unison the prayer on page 173.

6. Have different group members read aloud a consecutive verse each from Matthew 4:1-11. Ask: What strikes you most about this encounter? Do you think the devil did this only to Jesus, or that he does it to all humans, albeit more subtly? If Satan were to ask you these questions (without knowing what Jesus did), how do you think you would have responded? Would you or the devil have won this skirmish?

7. The phrase 'the Word of God' entails that God is a speaking, communicating God. Have different group members read aloud a consecutive verse each from Genesis 1:1-10; John 1:1-5; and 1 John 1:1-4. Discuss how the three passages reflect and amplify one another.

8. Have the parents in the room reflect on the experience of teaching their children how to talk. How did speech lead to 'object permanence' for their children, as Rick discussed on page 185? How does God's speech relate to our assurance that God truly exists, that is to say, has 'object permanence'?

9. Ask: How many people remember the days of DOS and computers? Was it easy or difficult to install programs? Discuss: How is Scripture, in Rick's terminology, 'self-installing'?

10. Discuss various methods of reading and saturating oneself with Scripture, so that it can self-install in our minds, bodies, hearts and even souls.

11. Discuss the difference between *logos* and *rhema*. Why is this important for Christians to understand? What is a danger some believers run into when saying, "The Lord told me..."?

12. Ask if members desire to commit to simple daily disciplines, such as reading a chapter or two of the Bible a day, or listening to the Bible on CD as they commute to work, in order to put more of God's Word in their hearts in a regular, systematic way?

13. Turn to Appendix One, "Friday" (page 263). Ask each person to consecutively read a prayer aloud. One member at a time, go around the circle and ask each person to try to pray a prayer, substituting the name and rephrasing the pronouns as necessary.

14. **Homework** for next week: "My Favorite Prayer" contest. Ask each group member to bring a copy of his/her 'favorite prayer,' and be ready to describe why it is so meaningful for them. For example, the *Serenity Prayer* may have helped someone overcome an addiction, the *Apostle's Creed* may remind another person of their childhood church, and the *Prayer of Saint Francis of Assisi* may have helped yet another person integrate faith and a love of nature. (Suggest they bring several copies to share, if they are able.)

15. Decide who will bring the next week's gifts. Close in prayer.

Week Eight:

Saturday: Steadfastly Pray in the Spirit

Scripture:

"And pray in the Spirit on all occasions with all kinds of prayers and requests. With this in mind, be alert and always keep on praying for all the saints."

(Ephesians 6:18)

Group Instructions & Study Questions:

1. Show and Tell: ask group members to read aloud the 'favorite prayer' they brought to share and describe why it is so meaningful for them.

    Rather than voting for the best prayer, maybe the group leaders would choose this night to give a final gift to each member, such as a bookmark with the Lord's Prayer.

2. Before beginning the lesson, continue last week's discussion as to whether the group intends to end or carry on with a new study. If you all decide to carry on, you need to finalize which topic or book of the Bible the group will study.

3. Open with a prayer that God would help each member of the group learn how to better protect those they love, through the keys given in Ephesians 6.

4. Read Ephesians 6:18 aloud and in unison (see above).

5. Have each person turn to Chapter Eight of *How to Protect Those You Love (By Praying the Armor of God)*. Begin by praying aloud and in unison the prayer on page 204.

6. Ask: Are you a workaholic? Why or why not? Would your spouse agree with your answer? Your boss or coworkers? Your pastor?

7. Ask: Are you good at taking vacations? Why of why not? What is the best vacation you have ever taken? What was the most restful?

8. Discuss the historical fact that Yahweh, the God of Israel, is the only deity in all of known history who is regarded by his followers as having commanded them to *rest*. Brainstorm the possible reasons that Yahweh might have had behind the commandment to rest.

9. When is your Sabbath? When do you take a break, kick up your feet, and rest? Do you find activity or inactivity more restful? Why

10. Some Christians sleep in on Sundays because it is their "only day

to rest." Do you think this is a valid reason for missing church?

11. Ask: Do you consider yourself good at praying? Why or why not? Also ask: Would you like to become better at praying? If so, what is holding you back?

12. Have different group members read aloud a consecutive verse each from Psalm 25:1-2; Psalm 32:10; Psalm 56:3-4; and Ephesians 5:18-19.

13. Try the prayers suggestions on page 217-218. For each prayer, have each group member pray that prayer specifically for someone he/she loves.

14. Have each group member discuss a difficult situation or person he/she is currently dealing with. Then ask, With whom do you discuss this situation most: yourself, others, or God? Ask: How might *Rick's rule for prayer* be applied in your situation?

15. Discuss the assurance we Christians have that, no matter how difficult or sorrowful this world may be, we will have perfect and eternal rest for our souls in heaven. Ask each member to discuss one earthly burden that he/she is looking forward to being relieved of in heaven.

16. Turn to Appendix One, "Saturday" (page 267). Ask each person to consecutively read a prayer aloud. One member at a time,

go around the circle and ask each person to try to pray a prayer, substituting the name and rephrasing the pronouns as necessary.

17. **Homework** for next week: If the group is continuing, specify the relevant Bible passage they are to read in preparation, or if the topic is book-led, the relevant chapter they are to read. (Hand out copies of the book for purchase, if available.)

18. Close in prayer, asking each person to pray a prayer of spiritual protection for the other members of the group, using whatever item of armor they desire to pray for the group as a whole. In this manner, the group will end with a unified effort to 'protect those we love by praying on the armor of God.'

Acknowledgements

"I thank my God every time I remember you" (Philippians 1:3)

- Gay Stedman, mother extraordinaire, to whom this book is dedicated.
- Don Stedman, my father, for his never-ending support and encouragement through all the escapades of my life.
- My precious wife Amy, the love and joy of my life.
- Our three beloved children: Micah, Noah, and Jesse. Now that you all are in college, may God protect you with his armor every day. Also, as you move out from our home and establish your own homes and families, may you walk in his paths of joy and blessing all the days of your lives.
- My in-laws Dean and Marcia Holst, my siblings Randy & Teri, and the rest of our extended family too numerous to name, thank you for the joys of family that you give to us.
- Our church, Adventure Christian Church of Roseville, California. You are the best! I truly love you and love being your pastor.
- The number one administrative assistant in the world: Lori Clark. I could not have done this—or any other part of my ministry—without your help.
- Our church staff and elders: thank you for the privilege of serving with you as co-laborers in the Lord's kingdom. Special thanks to our elders who unfailingly protect, challenge

and encourage me: Bryce Jessup, Bill Twelker, Randy Blair, Frank Nitto, Ken Oosting, Mike Edwards, Brad Dacus, Steve McNally, and Rick Perez.

- Special thanks also to our church staff directors, who so capably oversee their ministry areas and thus free me to do mine: Gil Stieglitz, Laurie Kelley, Heidi Coughran, Melody Hussein, Renee Flores, Lydia Khachadourian, Anthony Harrison, and Kyle Hedwall.

- Last but certainly not least, to my superb editing team: Nicholas Domich, Glenn Ellis, Bev Graham, Vivian Jones, Jeff Olson, Phil Otte, Carol Peterson, Alan Reinhart, Steve Rindfuss, and Julia Staton. Thanks for all the time, effort, and expertise you have given to this project. I'm so thankful God brought each of you, and your distinct talents, into my life. This is your book too, and it is my prayer that our efforts will help many Christians find the protection they so desperately need in this evil world. SDG.

CPSIA information can be obtained at www.ICGtesting.com
Printed in the USA
LVOW090356170312

273337LV00002B/1/P